The Millennium Planner

THE
MILLENNIUM
PLANNER

Your Personal Guide to the Year 2000

Peter Lorie

VIKING STUDIO BOOKS

A LABYRINTH BOOK

VIKING
STUDIO
BOOKS

VIKING STUDIO BOOKS

Published by the Penguin Group
Penguin Books USA Inc., 375 Hudson Street, New York, New York 10014, U.S.A.
Penguin Books Ltd, 27 Wrights Lane, London W8 5TZ, England
Penguin Books Australia Ltd, Ringwood, Victoria, Australia
Penguin Books Canada Ltd, 10 Alcorn Avenue, Toronto, Ontario, Canada M4V 3B2
Penguin Books (N.Z.) Ltd, 182-190 Wairau Road, Auckland 10, New Zealand

Penguin Books Ltd, Registered Offices: Harmondsworth, Middlesex, England

First published in 1995 by Viking Penguin,
a division of Penguin Books USA Inc.

1 3 5 7 9 10 8 6 4 2
Copyright © Peter Lorie, 1995
Original illustrations copyright © Malcolm Godwin, 1995
Illustration credits appear on page 122
All rights reserved

Produced by Labyrinth Publishing (UK) Ltd
Typesetting by Moonrunner Design, England
Designed by Malcolm Godwin
Printed in Italy
Library of Congress in Publication Data *available upon request*

ISBN 0-670-85682-7

CONTENTS

INTRODUCTION

USING THE PLANNER (6)

Your Personal Prophet Center (6) – The Calendar (10)
– Letter to the Future (12) – Sourcing the Future (14)

THE PROPHECIES (28)

The Jubilee Year 2000 (28) – The Christ-Center (36) – The Future of War (48)
– George Washington's Vision (52) – The Prophetic Pyramid & the End of the World (56)
– Future-Quakes & Other Prophecies of Edgar Cayce (68)
– Jeane Dixon—Living Prophet (76) – The Sibylline Oracles (82)
– The Future of God (86) – How Many Humans? (90) – Citification (95)
– Economic Apocalypse (98) – Woman-Power (102) – Family Futures (110)

BIBLIOGRAPHY (116)

Acknowledgments

INTRODUCTION

USING THE PLANNER

Your Personal Prophet Center

O N DECEMBER 31, 1999, AT MIDNIGHT, A DAY, A MONTH, A YEAR, A DECADE, A CENTURY AND A MILLENNIUM WILL END. The last time this happened—a thousand years ago—the world underwent convulsions of insecurity and doubt in the expectation of numerous disasters and changes. It was believed then, as it still is in many places, that the world would come to an end. But *The Millennium Planner* has other ideas.

The pages of this book contain a broad selection of predictions from some of the world's most successful prophets, past and present, that tell us that the year 2000 and the beginning of the twenty-first century is likely to be an extraordinary time of change, both joyful and troubled, with much to make up for the problems of the twentieth century.

Of course, the future can never be all positive and rosy. There are bound to be problems, for this is the nature of life. Perhaps, though, if we know something of the future in advance we may feel better prepared. Taken from the works of St. John, Nostradamus, Malachy, Edgar Cayce, Jeane Dixon and contemporary economic and political forecasters, the text and illustrations set out to give us a picture of the year 2000.

Above: *Michel de Nostradame, the sixteenth-century prophet. Although this book includes only a few of the prophecies of Nostradamus, his influence down the ages, upon prophets and seers, has been greater than any other.*

Opposite: *Detail of an eighteenth-century* **Map of the Universe**, *from the British Museum in London.*

7

Opposite: *The frontispiece to* **Raphael's Witch** *or "Oracle of the Future," published in 1831, showing the Wheel of Pythagoras, a device used in numerical fortune-telling.*

Above: *One of the many popular images created in the earlier part of this century to depict the prophetic capabilities of oracles. Note the ghost-like emanations from the center of the earth beneath the chair of the oracle. Convenient steps are provided for her to take the occasional break!*

But *The Millennium Planner* is not simply a package of predictions, for it can also bring personal good fortune to many readers, perhaps to you, as you turn the pages right now. For contained within the words and illustrations on these pages, and within the other items provided in the pack, there is a competition. This competition consists of a number of specific questions related to the years between 1996 and 2000, each concerned with details of events or situations that are likely to occur in the up-coming years, the last years of the twentieth century. How many people will there be on earth in the future, for example? Where will the wars be fought? How many women will there be in positions of power? Who will be the US president after the next elections? Readers can become prophets, and the most successful will win substantial prizes. A new edition of *The Millennium Planner* will be published each year starting in 1995, with a new set of questions related to the following year's potential statistics or events. Each year the "Prophet of the Year" will be chosen from the entrants and each year a prize will be awarded to the winner or winners.

Look inside the slipcase alongside the book to find the contest leaflet with the questions for this year. Send in your answers by the date specified and maybe win a great prize.

So become your own Prophet Center and enter the competition each year, starting now, for the prizes are waiting for the successful entrants.

The atmosphere of the Earth is overloaded with chemicals which trap the heat of the sun's rays, blanketing our atmosphere, creating the infamous greenhouse effect. The temperature of the Earth is rising faster than anything known since the last ice age. Sea levels will rise world-wide, and some island nations will be entirely submerged. *This global warming may, inadvertently, prevent the predicted, catastrophic wobble of the planet caused by the build-up of ice in the Antarctic, and the line-up of the planets on May 5th 2000.*

Also in the box is the very first full-color calendar for the year 2000. Illustrated with original imagery which represents the future, and with space for your anticipated appointments and anniversaries, this gorgeous calendar is designed to give readers a sense of how the year 2000 will be. Write in your birthdate, anniversaries of loved ones and special dates—including the date when you can expect to win the prize. Then keep the calendar safely until the time that it begins—on January 1—the first day of the twenty-first century—the "third millennium."

Above: *An illustration showing the planetary line-up which will occur on May 5th in the year 2000.*

Letter to the Future

And finally, there is a specially designed letter to the future. You can write details of your personal predictions for the year 2000—your expectations of employment, your annual income, how many children you will have, whether you expect to be married or single, and where you might be living—together with your answers to the questions in the competition. You can also record details of your life now, as a personal historical document for the future. Write down your own personal predictions and memories and seal the document, keep it safely until the year 2000 and then open it and see just how accurate your predictions were.

But let us now delve into the future and open the doors to what promises to be an incredible new millennium.

Above: *Detail of the Star Chart from the domed ceiling of the Frederiksborg Palace, Hillrød, Denmark, showing mythological representations of the heavens.* Opposite: *The artist Erich Schrempp's rendering of **Infinity** as an endless series of open doors.*

Sourcing the Future

There have been literally hundreds of prophets in our past. They have come in many different forms - "seers," scientists, clairvoyants, astrologers, masters and gurus, popes, madmen and cranks. And all of them, in some way or another, have claimed to be able to see into the future. But only a handful have remained well known to us today - Nostradamus, Edgar Cayce, St. John the Divine, Malachy, and a few others. And each age produces its own prophets; the more troubled the era, the more prophets appear. The twentieth century has had its own share, a few of them in recent years, such as Edgar Cayce, the American prophet who still surprises the world with the success of his predictions, and Jeane Dixon, who will almost certainly live to see the accuracy or otherwise of her predictions for the year 2000.

There have also been whole nations that believed in prophetic teaching - the Jewish prophets, for example, and the Atlanteans and Egyptians, who built the pyramids, it is believed, at least in part to provide mankind with a picture of the future. It seems that some people have a gift for getting in touch with aspects of our surroundings that are not commonly available to the rest of us. It is as though there is a crack in existence through which a few specially gifted individuals can look, while the rest of us remain blind. Each of these prophets of our past have used different "tools" and techniques, ranging from contact with spirits through clairvoyance, water reading, herbal trances, meditation, automatic writing, to astrology.

There are certain ages and conditions in which the visions of past prophets seem to become more popular. We pay attention to magic when we are afraid of the current reality. When life appears to be traveling

MICHEL NOSTRADAMUS

Since his death in the late sixteenth century, Nostradamus' works, originally entitled The Centuries, *have never been out of print. As we draw closer to the end of the millennium, so we see more and more editions appearing. Most of the fears engendered by the end-of-millennium scenario are Christian-based, and much of Nostradamus' prophecies was also born of this same religious conditioning.*

EDGAR CAYCE

One of our most recent, and one of only two major American prophets, Edgar Cayce, made most of his prophecies while in a state of trance. Many of them have proven accurate, and many more have yet to come to pass. Perhaps the most significant are those directed at the beginning of the twenty-first century

uncontrollably forward in directions we may not understand, we turn to the occult, the mystical, and particularly visions of the future, to find comfort. It is also true that we are attracted to and stimulated by the unknown or irrational. Take our current interest in the most famous prophet of them all - Nostradamus. How does such an individual apply his gift for seeing, not only into his own immediate future, but thousands of years into our future?

Michel de Nostradame, born in the first few years of the sixteenth century, was trained as a doctor of medicine in the South of France. As a young man he was taught the secrets of the occult and the rituals of ancient learning by his grandfather and his uncle, who were part of the French court of King Francis I. His family had been Jewish, but was forced to convert to Christianity in order to avoid the horrors of the Spanish Inquisition. Any ritual or persuasion that followed practices derived from pagan (pre-Christian) beliefs was banned, and the punishment for anyone caught or even believed to be involved in such practices was violent death - burning at the "stake."

Nostradamus (the Latin form of his name) showed astonishing gifts of prophecy from early in his life. Stories are told of events occurring while he traveled throughout France with his grandfather and uncle, in which he displayed these gifts, and later when he was escaping the Spanish Inquisitors who sought him for his heretical occult practices. On one occasion he met a simple traveling monk on the road. Nostradamus stopped the monk and kneeled before him, kissed his hand and addressed him as "Your Holiness"– a term used only for the Pope. The monk actually became Pope some forty years later.

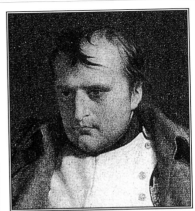

People related to Nostradamus' most successful prophecies. Opposite, top left to bottom right: **Henry II** *of France whom Nostradamus predicted would die of a wound through his helmet;* **Napoleon Bonaparte**, *the "second anti-Christ;"* **John F. Kennedy**, *"The great man stuck down by a thunderbolt;"* **Pope John Paul I**, *whose short reign Nostradamus predicted exactly;* **Adolf Hitler**, *known as "Hister" in the prophecies; "the nine set apart...their fate determined on departure," the astronauts who died in the 1986* **Challenger** *disaster;* **President de Gaulle** *of France, "for three times one surnamed de Gaulle will lead France." Above:* **Robespierre**, *whom Nostradamus called the "fox" and the "tyrant" of the predicted French Revolution;* **Catherine de Medici**, *the fate of whose children the prophet accurately predicted; and finally* **Nostradamus** *himself.*

As he grew older this extraordinary seer began to write down the results of visions seen while in trance, which were eventually compiled into ten volumes of verses called *The Centuries*. As an old man he would undertake these strange trances and meditations in the top rooms of his house in Salon, southern France, and by candlelight dip into the astonishing realms of the future. Almost a thousand verses have been handed down to us, each one containing secret coded prophecies which have continued to reveal remarkably accurate pictures of the future for the four hundred years since his death.

During most of the twentieth century the works of Nostradamus have constantly remained in print in many different editions, with numerous interpretations, most of them extremely depressing. Pick up almost any paperback book on the subject, and you will find it burgeoning with disaster, death, disease, and catastrophe. The interpreters seem largely to see only "end-of-the-world" scenarios—Armageddon around every corner. There is very little difference between this response to life and that which existed at the end of the last millennium when everyone spoke of the Last Judgment—which of course never came. But humans are always forgetful and ready for the next Last Judgment! There is also that phenomenon, "Millenniamania," that has begun to strike the world even in the years before 1999, which will no doubt grow stronger as we approach the end of the century.

Left: ***The Tibetan Wheel of Life and Death***, *from the British Museum in London. The Tibetans believe life to be a cyclic event, with death simply like a comma in a long sentence.*

Opposite: ***A mother and child*** *from Somalia, amongst the millions of unfortunates who have a direct and daily experience of the "Age of Pain."*

As individuals we are constantly expecting the worst: tomorrow, next week, next month. So as a social group we are the same—disaster, doom etc. "A thousand fears and nothing ever happens." We forget—this is the beginning of the Age of Aquarius. And truly, not all Nostradamus's predictions are of disaster and doom, and neither are those of other prophets from our past.

According to the Hindu sages of India, humanity passes through seven cycles of existence, called *Mahayugas*, each one made up of seven *yugas*. The first *yuga*, which lasted for 1,728,000 years, was the age of perfection, whereas the fourth and most degenerate *yuga*, which began in 3102 BC, has continued as the *Kali Yuga*, or the Yuga of Pain. Is it possible that we might be at the very end of this stage of existence? Perhaps we have been in "the Age of Pain" for so long that we have forgotten what it is like to be out of pain. Certainly almost fifty-one centuries would seem to be enough to achieve major forgetfulness. According to Nostradamus and several other prophets, this may well be the case. Perhaps we really are in for a good time.

For it is possible to interpret almost anything as bad. If we look superficially, with our pessimistic

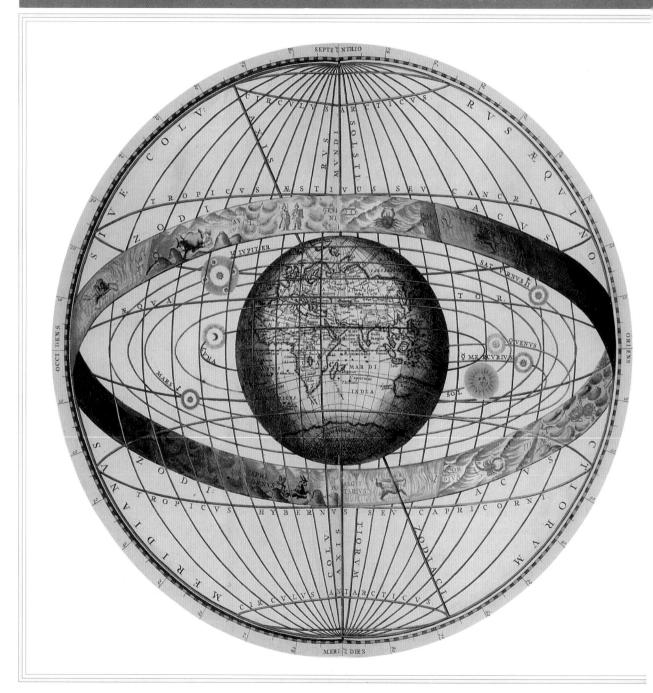

SCORPIO   LIBRA   VIRGO

SAGITTARIUS

LEO

RICORN

CANCER

AQUARIUS

GEMINI

PISCES

TAURUS

ARIES

eyes, at the texts of Nostradamus, Edgar Cayce, and St. John's Revelation, we find pretty quickly that we are looking through tears of sadness, when in fact, if we look just a little more carefully, we can actually turn those tears into tears of laughter, for the future is far from a time of doom.

But what about overpopulation, poverty and famine, political conflict and confusion, pollution, crime, fraud in official administrations, incompetent politicians, etc.—isn't all this getting worse? Aren't we looking at a future that will hold steadily growing problems of this nature? Or is there another explanation?

*Opposite: Detail from the **Map of the World According to Brahe**. Above: **The Zodiac**. As the earth orbits around the sun we change the backdrop of stars which can be seen when the sun rises. The sun has a longer cycle in which it passes through each of the signs of the zodiac approximately once every two thousand years.*

Because we tend to think so much in the short term—our lives, after all, are relatively short—we fail very often to see the longer-term cycles. One of the ways these can be understood is through astrology. Right now, in the broader cycle of human evolution we are in what is known as a "cusp" between different overriding signs of the global zodiac. Most of us are familiar with our birth signs. We may have a birthday on a date which is midway between two signs—perhaps on the 22nd of the month, or thereabouts. This means that we are subject to the influences of two different astrological signs. Just as each of us has a "star" sign,

*Right: Detail from **The Last Judgment**, by Hieronymus Bosch. All millennium and even century ends raise the specter of the Christian Last Judgment.*

so, on a grander scale, the movement of the planet Earth and all its inhabitants also has a governing sign. But in the case of the planetary signs, the changes happen on a much larger scale—once every two thousand years or so. We are, in the late twentieth century, at the center of the "change-over" between two different signs—Pisces and Aquarius. The sign of Pisces has governed planet Earth since approximately AD 50—the time when Christian thought began to influence the world. In fact, the beginning of the Age of Pisces was the beginning of Christianity. And this is highly significant, because the Age of Pisces was the age of blind belief, of unquestioning religious faith, of a belief in miracles and magic as the very foundation of life. This naturally gave birth to religious dogma to be obeyed by all. And with this concept of blind belief came much of the pessimism to which we have now become so accustomed.

The concept of the "Second Coming," the new arrival of the Messiah, grew out of the Piscean ideal of external realization—i.e. that everything relied upon an other-worldly force which was epitomized by God, all-powerful entity. During the Piscean Age, which is now coming to an end, humanity was seen as following God and the Church. Because individual volition was subject to the judgment of God, a human being had no power to influence his or her own future. God was the answer to everything, and the Church on Earth acted as his director, so to speak, offering guidance and laws which had to be obeyed, for man knew nothing of himself and therefore contained no power to operate without the aid of the deity.

The entire basis of all past prophetic writing, and much present for that matter, is the belief in the need to purify the human spirit. The whole basis of alchemical practices in the Middle Ages was this same desire for purification, in this case of base metal into gold and the use

The young generation born into the age of pollution knows nothing of a time when the world was pollution-free. Only the older amongst us can remember "fresh air." But then that generation experienced the "pollution" of the ghastly wars at the beginning of this century.

of the Philosopher's Stone, all intended as a kind of metaphor for human enlightenment.

The Book of Revelation in the Bible was provided as a kind of directive from God, seeming to show, inevitably, complete global pandemonium; an apocalyptic disaster in which humans who were essentially sinful would die in the apocalypse and only those who were pure of heart would survive to people the "New Jerusalem" that would result. The biblical flood was a precursor of this, bringing water to drown out the sins of mankind and allowing only Noah and his family and animals to return to the dry surface and begin again.

This biblical purgation myth is echoed in many other cultures—in Native American stories, for example, which tell of a world into which mankind arrived, sinned and then was expelled, leaving the pure of heart to begin again.

The Piscean Age is in its very last stages. We are at the onset of the Aquarian Age, which speaks to us much more of individual awakening—of the perfection of each human being through a process of spiritual alchemy which turns our individual psyches towards the same heaven referred to in the Bible and all other prophetic works, but on Earth, through an understanding of our natures.

So we are moving, at least from the point of view of astrological predictions, into a time of much greater joy and positivity.

Another, more local reason for the apparent disastrous nature of the environment of the late twentieth century is the astrological presence

The Golden Rock of Burma *that sits on*
the edge of oblivion and the abyss.

of the passing planet Pluto. Pluto, during the 1980s and 1990s, has been in transition through the sign of Scorpio, something that occurs only once in every two and a half centuries or so. It last occurred at the end of the fifteenth century, around the time of the birth of Nostradamus and the advent of the Renaissance period in Europe. This was the time of the Spanish Inquisition, and of the dreadful plague that swept across large parts of Europe and killed millions of people—rather similar in a sense to the plague of AIDS that we are now experiencing. Nostradamus, in fact, made direct reference to the effects of this planetary influence:

Then the impurities and abominations will be brought to the surface and made manifest...towards the end of the change in reign.

Interpreters have suggested that in this verse Nostradamus may have been referring to the change in the royal reign between Queen Elizabeth II and Charles of England.

When he writes of *the impurities and abominations* being *brought to the surface and made manifest* Nostradamus is referring to the effect that Pluto has as a kind of detoxifying power to bring poisons to the surface, rather like a sick body which kicks violently, the last vibrations before transformation and better health. In our age, this transformation is happening on a global scale. Humanity is undergoing the worst wars, the most violent political changes, the greatest effects of pollution, the most powerful natural disasters, because it is entering the closest proximity it has ever experienced to a transformation—to the new age of Aquarius. This is what all our past prophets have been trying to tell us, but we, in our Piscean state of pessimism, influenced by the passing of the Plutonian detoxifier, see it all as doom and gloom, when in fact what is really happening is the beginning of something incredibly exciting, extraordinarily beautiful and powerful. And that is the essence of the prophecies we are about to taste in the rest of this book.

THE
PROPHECIES

THE JUBILEE YEAR 2000

EVENTS around us point the way to an extraordinary and exciting future where many of the laws and rules that have been laid down by science and technology will be broken during the next generations. According to almost all of the prophets, much that is sure in the twentieth century will become unsure in the twenty-first. Anyone who today utters statements of absolute certainty had better be ready to change trains in the next ten years—especially the scientists.

And for those of us that believe it is not worth considering the future at all, because we won't be there, keep in mind that almost all the most famous prophets understood life to be a cyclic affair—not only within the one life but through many many lives. This has been written about and believed in for thousands of years.

The *Papyrus Anana*, a prophetic work written by the Chief Scribe of the Egyptian Pharaoh Jentle Leti II in 1300 BCE, gives us a most fascinating beginning to our vision of the next millennium:

Read, O children of the future and learn the secrets of the past which to you is so far away, and yet truth is so near.

Men do not live once only to depart hence forever, they live many times in many places, though not only in this world.

That between each life is a veil of darkness. The doors will be

Opposite: *City of the Future*, an illustration from the 1930s showing what was believed then to be the city of the year 2000. The future is seldom how it is imagined to be.

open at last to show us all the chambers through which our feet wandered from the beginning.

Our religion teaches us that we live eternally... now eternity, having no end, can have no beginning; it is a circle. Therefore if one be true, namely that we live on forever, it would seem that the other must be true also... namely, that we have always lived.

To men's eyes God has many faces and each swears that the one he sees is the only true God, yet they are all wrong, for all are true...

The strength of the invisible time will bind souls together long after the world is dead. In the end, however, all the various pasts will reveal themselves.

So if we can all expect to be present in the futures we foresee, either in this life or another, we might want to learn the art of the positive, the art of creative excitement, for the world has had plenty of disaster and doom. And even though there is still more to come, there is much also to look forward to, and even the most doomy of religious prophecies predicts a change for the better in the year 2000.

Egyptian scribe with papyrus scroll. This fourth-dynasty limestone statue from Sakkara exemplifies the contemplative aspect of magic and prophecy. We often see Egyptian representations in the squatting position, for meditation was a normal everyday practice.

State is the name of the coldest of all cold monsters.
Coldly it tells lies too; and this lie crawls out of its
mouth: "I, the state, am the people." This is a lie!
It is annihilators who set traps for the many and call
them "state": they hang a sword and a hundred appetites over
them...the state tells lies in all the languages of good and evil;
and whatever it says it lies—and whatever it has it has stolen.
Nietzsche—THUS SPAKE ZARATHUSTRA.

All end-of-millennium, judgment-day, second-coming religious expectations were originally born out of the Hebrew linear concept of time and history. Within Judeo-Christian tradition, the number seven took the central role in this process. Seven represented the vibration of harmony. The first feast day was the day on which God rested after the six days of Creation. There were seven ages of man, seven days in the week, seven major religious festivals during the year.

The Hebrew theory of time—known as the *Shemitah*—was based on seven cycles each of seven periods, just as the week is seven days and the year split, for the Hebrew people, into seven lots of seven days (forty-nine) with the fiftieth day being the Sabbath day. On the greater cycle

Friedrich Wilhelm Nietzsche—one of
our greatest gurus and philosophers,
some would say, even an enlightened
man. His observations on the nature of
"state" give pause to those of us who still
accept our rulers as just and right.

31

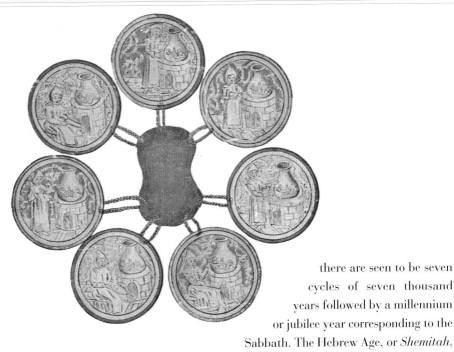

there are seen to be seven cycles of seven thousand years followed by a millennium or jubilee year corresponding to the Sabbath. The Hebrew Age, or *Shemitah*, that has influenced us, according to the Judaic beliefs, throughout this century has been an age of stern judgement. But in the year 2000 it ends, and with it the prohibitions, the sternness, will end also. A time of perfection will begin. This is at the very core of the Jewish struggle to return to Israel, in time for the next *Shemitah*, to greet the messiah who will appear, it is believed, following a terrible struggle, to redeem the world.

This Jewish apocalypse underlies all western religious belief, for devout Christians also expect an apocalypse that will lead to a promised utopia. And the timing is the same, popularly ending in the year 2000.

In St. John's Book of Revelation at the end of the New Testament, we are told the story of an apocalyptic crescendo of poisoning pollution, war, political mistrust, disease, and famine, followed by the dawning of a new age and an Aquarian heaven on Earth.

Opposite: *Ultra-orthodox Jews praying at the **Wailing Wall** in Jerusalem. Many of the Christian doom-laden scenarios were seeded by the Judaic tradition, without having any redeeming humor to offset the expectation of imminent catastrophe.*

Above: ***The Seven Processes*** *of the medieval alchemist, linked to the central, red, Philosopher's Stone.*

Above right: **Apocalypse: the dragon bound and cast into the bottomless pit.** *From an illuminated manuscript made during the thirteenth century, inspired by the Revelation of St. John the Divine.* Opposite: *The archangel Michael battles with "that old serpent." From the illuminated manuscript* Les Très Riches Heures du Duc de Berry.

And I saw an angel come down from heaven, having the key of the bottomless pit and a great chain in his hand.

And he laid hold on the dragon, that old serpent, which is the Devil, and Satan, and bound him a thousand years,

And cast him into the bottomless pit, and shut him up, and set a seal upon him, that he should deceive the nations no more, till the thousand years should be fulfilled: and after that he must be loosed a little season. REVELATION 20:1-3

Nostradamus tells the same story, in strikingly similar language:

Hearing the affliction of his people, God the creator will command that Satan be cast into the depths of the bottomless pit, and bound there. Then a universal peace will commence between God and man, and Satan will remain bound for around a thousand years...

The Christ~Center

CHRISTIANITY, therefore, of all the established religions, is the one most eager to celebrate the year 2000 with the new arrival of the Messiah. While the ancient traditions have taught, and still do teach in, for example, the Hindu beliefs, that life is a continuous cyclic process without end, Christianity has attempted to change the oldest conceptions of the world by giving history a kind of center, or mid-way-point. Time is considered finite, beginning at Creation and ending at the millennium—this millennium, and the year 2000. In doing this Christianity has lost the eternal quality of the ancient traditions because everything is seen to happen in time. The world is seen as a unique place with single, unrepeatable events instead of the more romantic and ever-lasting concepts of the eternal Greek gods and goddesses, or the Buddhist and Hindu religions, where we learn through many lifetimes of constantly returning cycles.

The date of the birth of Christ was the pivotal point, dividing history into everything that happened *before* his birth and the rest happening *after* it. In other words, everything that happened before Christ's birth was in preparation for the birth, and the rest was a preparation for his second coming. Dionysus Exiguus proposed the idea of using AD (Anno Domini) to delineate the time after Christ, in AD 525. Until that date the Roman calendar was in use, so that no one was particularly concerned with this linear approach, or the designation of Christ as the centerpoint of history. And it was not

The Last Judgement by Stephan Lochner, 1451. *The whole prophetic mode of Christianity starts with the Creation and ends with the Last Trump. The millennium fever which occurred in Europe a thousand years ago was fired by the belief that the end of the world was at hand.*

until 1681 that Bossuet proposed running the dates backwards for the time before Christ's birth. Until then, the years before Christ were simply not numbered at all.

Within the Islamic faith, there is a different starting date—1 Muharram, which was taken to be the date when Mohammed went from Mecca to Medina on July 16, 622 (Christian time). All years after 1 Muharram are given the suffix AH, which is short for Ab Hegira—"after the flight."

Christians believe, therefore, that because the birth of Christ was given the date AD 1, then the year 2000 is a potential major event as the two thousandth anniversary of Christ's birth, even though today it has become uncertain when he was actually born, the dates varying between 7 BC and AD 4.

The biblical prophets are said to have predicted all the events leading up to Christ's birth, and the Bible contains many predictions, particularly in the Book of Revelation, of events after Christ's birth and resurrection. One of these, perhaps most favored by Christianity, is the Second Coming, which many thousands of people believe to be due during the year 2000. Prior to the end of the first millennium after Christ, however, most Christians believed that the Second Coming would occur in the year 1000.

But the early biblical prophets were very successful in predicting events up to and including the birth of Jesus. In the eighth century before Christ, the prophet Isaiah predicted that Babylon, a rather small and poor state in his day, would grow into a powerful empire. He foretold that the armies of the emerging empire would overrun the land of Judah, reducing Jerusalem, its capital, to rubble:

Behold the days to come, that all that is in thine house, and that which thy fathers have laid up in store until this day, shall be carried to Babylon: nothing shall be left, saith the Lord. And of thy sons that shall issue from thee, which thou shalt beget, shall they

Opposite: ***The seven stages of human nature*** *within a cyclic framework. The alchemists were not enamored of the linear time frame of the orthodox Christian Church as it failed to fit with the ancient knowledge they had gained through generations of understanding. The picture is taken from the* Cabala *by Steffan Michelspacher, 1616.*

take away; and they shall be eunuchs in the palace of the king of Babylon. ISAIAH 39: 6-7.

And this whole land shall be a desolation, and an astonishment; and these nations shall serve the king of Babylon seventy years. JEREMIAH 25: 11

In fact history proved both these prophecies to be precisely right. After seventy years, the Medes and Persians led by Cyrus (whom the prophet Isaiah had named 200 years earlier) diverted the Euphrates River and marched along the watercourse to take the capital while Babylon was celebrating. Cyrus later released the Israelite prisoners who returned to their homeland to rebuild Jerusalem.

Many more of these early biblical predictions were fulfilled by history so that we perhaps might wish to read the predictions regarding our own time with some respect.

During the first centuries of Christianity there was a strong attraction to millennium-ends. The Book of Revelation provided, through the prophecies of St. John, the belief that the Second Coming would bring Christ and a new kingdom on Earth, reigned over directly by Christ himself for a thousand years (Ch. 20:4-6). The world would be peopled by Christian martyrs who were to be brought back to life after their persecution during the time before Christ returned as the Messiah. As early Christians believed themselves to be martyrs, the expectation was that Christ would appear at any minute.

The Book of Revelation is an extraordinary piece of apocalyptic writing that actually better represents the pagan than the Christian way of relating to the world, though it clearly has a direct relationship with the concept of Jesus Christ as the savior of

Cyrus, son of Cambyses, intended to make war on the Babylonians and become king of all Asia. When he arrived at the River Gyndes, he discovered he could not cross it on foot. When one of his special white horses was drowned, he swore to channel the river into 360 rivulets before attacking Babylon.

humanity, and tells a story which is intended to be prophetic of the future of Christianity. It is filled with astrology, alchemy, numerology, and very cryptic mysteries derived from Greek, Middle Eastern and Egyptian sources. It refers to concepts close to Eastern understanding, such as the seven *chakras*, and the seven letters to the churches of Asia at the beginning of the book have been interpreted (for example by George Gurdjieff) as metaphors for the growth of mankind towards enlightenment—a distinctly Eastern concept.

The story within Revelation seems particularly relevant to today, insofar as it can be seen as an apocalyptic prophetic work which suggests that the time before the Second Coming will be beset with terrible destruction, the collapse of all manner of human endeavor, and the eventual downfall of humanity before Christ arrives and puts everything right again—saving us all from ourselves. But, throughout history, since at least four hundred years after Christ's death, when Christianity actually began, the dating of the Second Coming has remained a singularly postponed event.

There has been, for example, the Apocalypse of Thomas, in which the Apostle Thomas was informed directly by Jesus that nine jubilees would pass between His ascension and the Second Coming:

On a sudden there shall arise near the last time a king, a lover of the law, who shall hold rule not for long: he shall leave two sons. The first is named with the first letter A, the second with the first letter H.

The prophecies go on to describe conflicts of various kinds, together with great floods, and then seven signs to humanity which would direct us to the end of the world and when it will occur. There are, amongst these signs, terrible diseases (AIDS, cancer, perhaps), poverty and starvation, natural disasters and voices from the heavens. Once all this has reached the final crescendo of disaster,

The Transfiguration, by Fra Angelico (c.1387-1455). Here is heralded the Second Coming of Christ, predicted to occur some time during the last four years of this century, depending on when you believe Christ was born.

The Great Fire of London of 1666—one of the events which was predicted and believed to herald the end of the world, in the Last Judgment. Probably because of ancient Judaic conditioning, humanity still prefers to predict, and report, negative events rather than positive ones.

those that Christ selects—i.e. good Christians—will be taken up into heaven, to rest there for eternity.

Various other works of prophecy, such as the Apocalypses of Peter and Paul, and the Revelation of Stephen, to name but a few, contain similar messages, and at numerous times in our recent history there have been cults, gatherings and groups who have followed the word of one declared messiah or another into various locations in Europe and the Middle East, to await the incarnation of Christ that would deliver them from this hell on Earth.

Montanus, for example, in the second century, declared himself the incarnation of the Holy Ghost, telling those who listened that the New Jerusalem, as predicted in Revelation, was at hand. Thousands of Montanists went to Phrygia, which lies between the Mediterranean and the Black Sea, to await the Second Coming.

There have been literally hundreds of attempts to predict the likely date of the Second Coming, using the numbers, the astrological details or other aspects of Revelation as the basis. The numbers 1260 and 666 have been most popularly employed, though now that those two dates are long gone, interpretations need to be more ingenious.

Millennial dates tend to be excellent recruiting devices for Christianity, for as the end of such a long era looms closer and closer, humanity has a tendency to fear it more and more. The Christians shortly before the year 1000 were still persecuted, but as the end of the millennium approached they became more popular, and numerous millennial cults emerged, such as the Ebonists and Montanists. Special laws were passed, such as those allowing specific leases that would end in the year 1000, so that tenants would not need to pay rent after the end of the world!

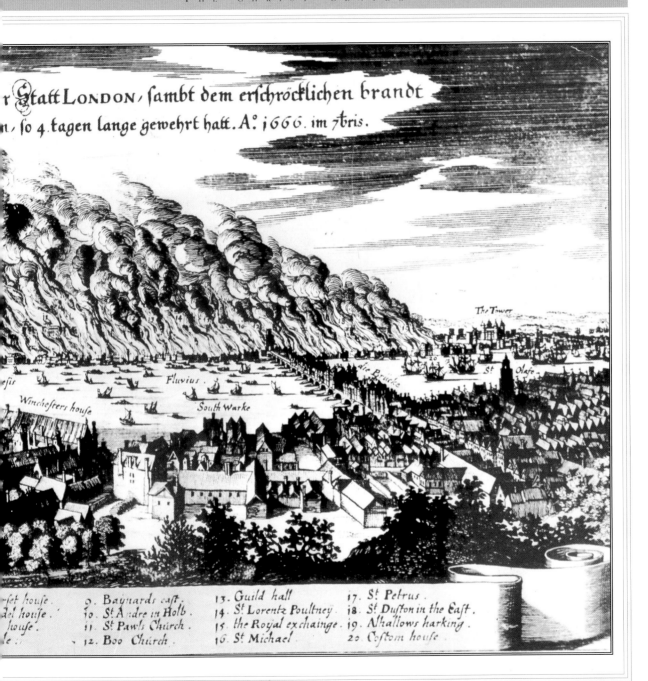

r Statt LONDON, sambt dem erschröcklichen brandt
n, so 4 tagen lange gewehrt hatt. A° 1666. im 7bris.

The Tower

Fluvius

die Brücke

St Olase

Winchesters house

South Warke

rset house.	9. Baynards cast.	13. Guild hall	17. St Petrus.
del house.	10. St Andre in Holb.	14. St Lorentz Poultney.	18. St Duston in the East.
house.	11. St Pawls Church.	15. the Royal exchainge.	19. Alhallows harking.
le.	12. Boo Church.	16. St Michael.	20. Costom house.

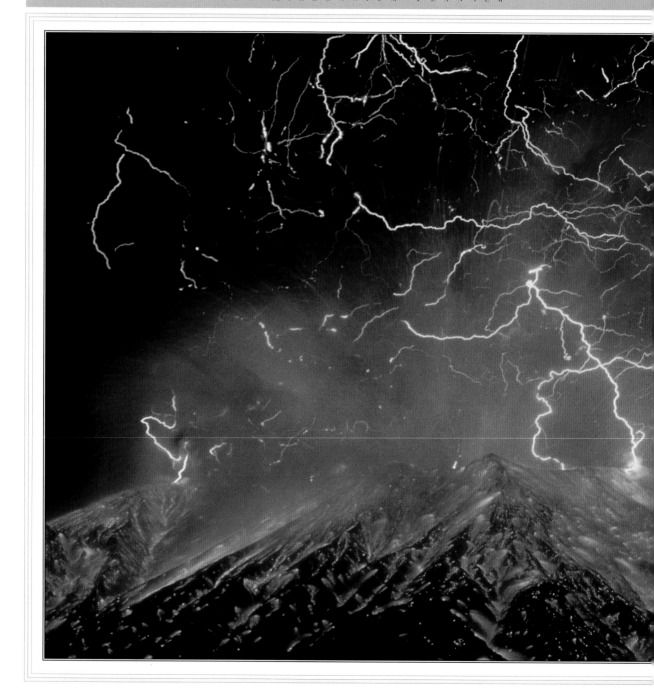

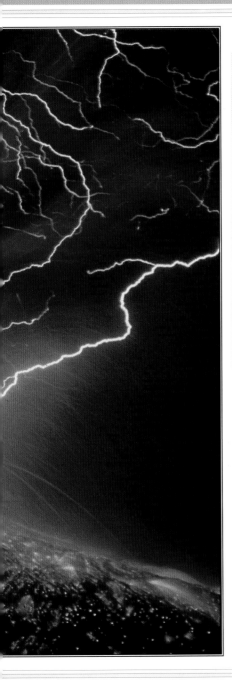

But the rivers did not turn to blood, nor did the devil walk through the countryside, nor dragons swoop down from the clouds. The year 1000 came and went, and we are all still here, as no doubt we will be in the year 2001.

Since then, there have been many more dates for the Second Coming—1033, 1496, 1524, 1656, and of course 1666 because of its link with the number of the beast—666—in Revelation. But only London burned during that year.

Many of the religions of the world—Judaism, Christianity, Native American, Islam—predict that just before the Last Judgment nations will go to war against one another, great earthquakes will proliferate across the globe, the Earth will shift its axis, mountains will move, cities and large areas of land will disappear beneath the waves, and new lands will rise up above them. All this will prologue the arrival of the Messiah. In verses of the Bible such as Luke 21:11, and Revelation 16:18, catastrophic events crash down upon Earth prior to the final fall:

And there were voices, and thunders, and lightnings; and there was a great earthquake, such as was not since men were upon the earth, so mighty an earthquake, and so great.

The fall then leads to a rebirth of humanity, and a new world that will be infinitely better than the previous one.

The year 2000 is probably the most powerful representation of that expectation yet to face humanity. We have the wars, the unrest, the earthquakes, the disasters, the general deterioration of the human condition. We have the year 2000 as the anniversary of the believed birth of Christ, and we have a strong revival of fundamentalist Christian belief. We can, according to all this, expect the end of the world to occur sometime during the year 2000.

An electrical storm around the edge of the constantly active volcano in Sakura-jima, Japan. According to most prophecies from our distant past, we are the generation that will actually face the apocalypse.

The Future of War

One of the ways in which the world might end is through war. According to a special issue of *The Economist* magazine, published at the end of 1993 and devoted to the end of the millennium, by the year 2000 we shall be looking at different patterns of war. During the earlier parts of the twentieth century wars were fought largely on an east-west axis between Germany, Russia, Italy, America, Britain, Japan and France. All the powers were in the northern hemisphere, and fought each other in attempts to gain greater territorial rights. During the first years of the twenty-first century, according to Brian Beedham, an associate editor and economic forecaster for *The Economist*, wars will be fought between north and south because of the increasing disparity between the stable powers in the northern hemisphere who won the wars of the twentieth century, and the increasingly unstable economies of the south, such as southern Asia and Africa, where

*The new **Eurofighter 2000** is designed and built by companies from four of the European nations—Britain, Italy, Germany and Spain. Increasingly the burden of research and development of advanced weaponry is too great to be borne by one nation alone. By the year 2000 it will be common practice amongst even the richest countries to "rent a gun." Already the British*

government is considering hiring equipment in a desperate attempt to keep down the escalating costs of maintaining a military presence. If this is the trend, then in a nightmare scenario we may expect the "mail order war barons" shortly to be in a position to offer nuclear devices to those who can pay.

many conflicts are growing. According to Beedham, one of the motivations for wars during the early years of the next millennium will be the differences between democratic and non-democratic countries. There are approximately 190 countries in the world, and some sixty of these are still not democratically run. Of these sixty countries, forty-five of them are in Africa and southern Asia, run by dictatorships with strong individual economic interests, and a determination to deny the populations the vote. The democratic countries of the world have become more willing in recent years to face up to thuggish leadership in non-democratic countries, so that wars may develop simply because of the increasing number of nations who rise above poverty through autocratic leadership.

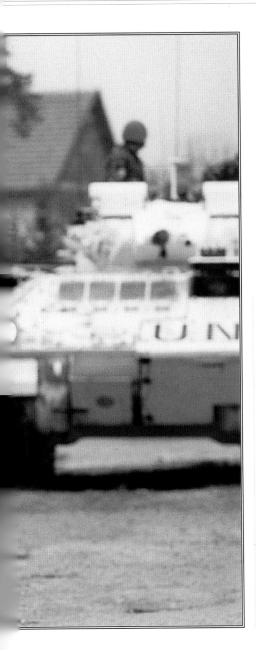

Bosnian refugees, 1993. The refugee problem in Europe overflows through a constant series of border disputes brought about in turn by the greed of our still powerful warlords. Either the end of the millennium will produce still more such problems or we will learn to end our passion for war.

According to Beedham, there are further likely reasons for war in the future. There is continued and increasing presence of multiracial conflict in countries that have not hitherto had many different ethnic groups within single borders, as well as in countries like the United States where ethnic minorities have become ethnic majorities. As peoples of the world migrate more freely, as minority group populations grow faster, and as dictatorships cause certain ethnic groups to flee their homelands, so other countries will have to face up to the problems of co-operation, or the lack of it, between different races. This was much of the reason behind the wars in the countries of what was formerly Yugoslavia, and we may see more of this kind of fighting amongst African nations during the next century.

The likely result of trends towards conflict in the twenty-first century will be a more closely formed alliance between the European nations and the United States, with a powerful and flexible army capable of dealing with bush-fire wars that spring up suddenly in a variety of different places.

George Washington's Vision

O ne of the most dramatic prophecies made during the history of the United States occurred in the offices of George Washington during one of the darkest years of the American Revolution.

Washington had given strict instructions to his staff not to interrupt his work on a particular day while he prepared a special dispatch. As he sat working he suddenly felt the presence of someone very powerful in the room with him, even though the doors and windows were shut against interruption. Looking up, he saw a woman of great beauty standing before him, her arm pointing towards the east. Washington thought that death had come to take him, and felt tremendous trepidation at the vision. The woman spoke the words: "Son of the Republic, look and learn." Turning towards where she indicated, Washington saw a great mist rising where the room's walls had been replaced with a distant scene. Spread out before him were America, Europe, Asia and Africa, with all the countries on a vast plain, and the oceans also visible. A dark shadow passed over it all and suspended itself directly between America and Europe, taking the form of a powerful, dark angel. This frightening entity threw water from the Atlantic Ocean over America with his right hand and over Europe with his left.

America was then completely engulfed in a huge cloud, and massive flashes of lightning were seen, followed by the cries of the inhabitants of the whole country.

Opposite: ***The Historical Monument of the American Republic,*** *by Erastus Salisbury Field.* Above: ***Noah's Ark,*** *by Joseph Hidley.* Right: ***George Washington as Grand Master.*** *Washington's vision of America was still that of a Noah's Ark—a fresh beginning in The New World. The year 2000 sees that Great American Dream confronted by the harsher realities of the modern world.*

The scene developed, and Washington watched as hundreds and thousands of towns sprang up all over the country. At this time there were only thirteen colonies in America, so that this vision of development on such an enormous scale was as futuristic and prophetic as any prophecy today that might tell us of an alien world.

The next scene was of a dark specter rising from Africa and moving to engulf America with its ill omen. Washington watched as it moved from town to town and through all the newly grown cities that he had just seen appear.

Next came another horrifying scene as each of the other countries of the world threw up another black cloud, this time with a red light at the center, through which Washington could see huge numbers of armed men marching by land and then traveling across the sea to envelop America completely.

Cities and lands were devastated by thundering cannons and clashing swords with shouts from millions of people in battle.

Eventually the cloud began to disperse as the angel once again sprinkled water from the oceans onto America, and the battle finally ceased.

The vision has been interpreted in several different ways, the most popular being that it foretold the Napoleonic Wars of 1812, the American Civil War and a massive invasion of the United States due to occur at the end of this millennium.

Another interpretation might be that the black cloud from Africa is AIDS, which partly originated in Africa, and which is currently devastating some sectors of the United States. The final onslaught seen by Washington is believed to be a prophecy of the first ever invasion of the United States, which, according to the Book of Revelation 9:13-16, could involve two hundred million men in combat just before the Last Judgment in the year 2000.

Opposite: *George Washington as a Freemason.* American contrasts: On the one hand we see the US absorbed by the high-minded concepts of human rights, while on the other we find the violence we cause through prejudices and fears related to ethnic minorities. Above: *The mystical symbol on the dollar bill is a favorite of the Freemasons, whose origins can be traced back to Hermetic magic and the secrets of the pyramids of Egypt.*

The Prophetic Pyramid and the End of the World

We really don't know when the Great Pyramid of Cheops, in Egypt, was built. There are theories that it is around four thousand years old, and that it was built for the Pharaoh Cheops, though this theory fails because there is no possible way that the Great Pyramid could have been built in any single lifetime. One other theory tells us that Cheops simply appropriated the pyramid as his tomb, in which case it could be thousands of years older. One of the most recent ideas related to this is that the pyramids and the Sphinx were actually built by the Atlanteans, and that Egypt was born out of Atlantis. In this case, which actually, when we look closely at the available history of Egypt, makes better sense, the Great Pyramid may be as much as nine thousand years old. One thing is sure, that even today, with the most sophisticated machinery and architectural engineering capability, it would be virtually impossible to construct a similar monument.

One of the most exciting aspects of the Great Pyramid is that it has been found to contain measurements which coincide exactly with certain events throughout our recent (the last two thousand years) history. In their book *Great Pyramid Passages*, John and Morton Edgar imposed a series of interpretations on the lengths of the passages that run through the center of the Great Pyramid. Their ideas gave birth to a fascinating concept.

The Great Pyramid of Cheops *at Giza, Egypt.*

Above right: *Antarctic Ice flow.* Inset: *The Southern Pole, showing the extent of the ice field.* Opposite: *According to the theory, as the ice builds up in the Antarctic, so it begins to affect the Earth's spin, causing a wobble which could be catastrophic when it coincides with the planetary line up in the year 2000.*

Archaeological investigators found that if they took one inch to signify one year of 365.242 days (the precise length of the solar year), the measurements within the chambers and passages of the Great Pyramid coincided so precisely with important events in our history that it seemed possible that those who built this monument were able to see into the future with astonishing accuracy. The date of the birth of Jesus, for example, was exactly measurable in one length of one chamber. And from the measurement of this date, going forward to the Hall of Truth in Light, one of the chambers inside the Great Pyramid, they made a measurement which brought them to April 7, AD 30 (Julian Calendar)—the date of the crucifixion. Other measurements took them to the beginning of World War I—1914, and then on to the exact date of the beginning of World War II, and finally to May 5, 2000. What, we may ask, is going to happen on May 5, 2000? If all the other dates have been accurate, perhaps this one will be also.

One of the most dramatic scenarios for this date arises from both astronomical projections and a theory related to the axis of the

The Tokyo earthquake of 1923 *almost completely leveled the town of Nihombushi.*

planet. According to recent projections, Antarctica's ice mass will by then be over three miles thick, perhaps even four miles. This may, it is suggested, be caused by changes in the climatic conditions of the planet in the last years of the twentieth century, heralding the beginning of a new ice age. If this were the case, it is proposed that such a massive weight on the planet's surface would potentially cause a "wobble" in the movement of the natural axis, that the Earth would slip into a different axis, and that this would coincide with planetary alignments due to occur during the year 2000.

Evidence of this alignment is brought to bear from assessments concluded at the Fernbank Science Center's Planetarium of Emory University in Atlanta, Georgia, which indicate that on that same precise date of May 5, 2000 there will be an exact line-up of various planets—Mercury, Venus, Earth, Mars, Jupiter and Saturn—and that such an unusual astronomical phenomenon might also herald an event of catastrophic proportions.

Movement of plate

PACIFIC PLATE

MAJOR CONTINENTAL PLATES

The areas which are most vulnerable to volcanic activity, earthquake and landshifts are those where the great continental plates meet. It is at these points, where one plate can either push over the other or shear away entirely, that any shift in the planetary axis could have disastrous consequences for those living near.

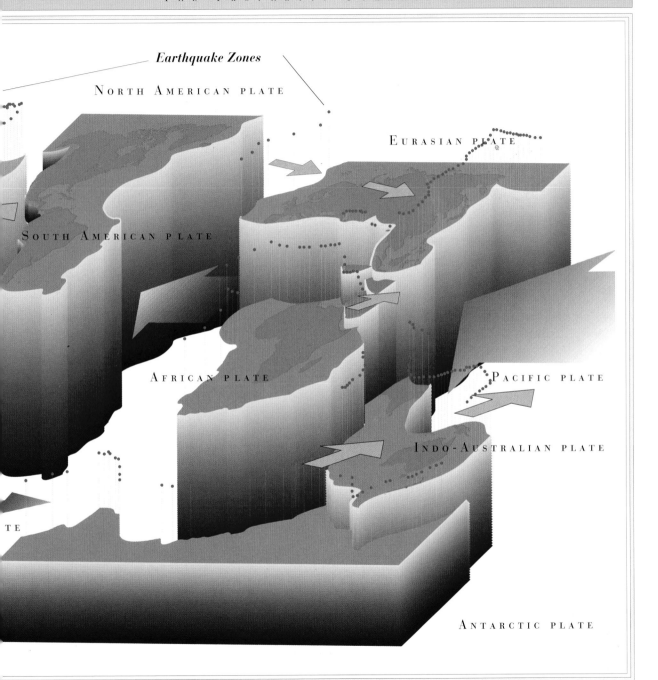

Earthquake Zones

NORTH AMERICAN PLATE

EURASIAN PLATE

SOUTH AMERICAN PLATE

AFRICAN PLATE

PACIFIC PLATE

INDO-AUSTRALIAN PLATE

TE

ANTARCTIC PLATE

The prediction that is concluded from these two events is that the tectonic plates on Earth will shift, causing massive earthquakes and climate changes which will bring the world to a shuddering and sudden end!

There are a number of predictions, made by several of the world's better known prophets, that point towards a series of major earthquakes, often called "superquakes" occurring during the year 2000.

One of the great favorites in this respect is, of course, Nostradamus, who predicted that:

An earthquake will be reported from the bottom of Asia... in an unstable and troubled state...(when) Mars, Mercury and the Moon are in conjunction.

The last time this planetary conjunction took place was October 1993, almost exactly the time of the superquake that killed 30,000 people on the Indian sub-continent.

Dr. Jeffrey Goodman, in his book *We are the Earthquake Generation*, predicted that the massive quakes would begin in 1987, and, in common with other prophets, Nostradamus suggests that the massive quake in India would be the beginning of a chain reaction of super-after-shocks that would ripple through Asia Minor, Greece and the West of Europe.

In another verse Nostradamus tells us:

For several nights the earth will shake, in the Spring two great efforts together; Corinth (Greece) and Ephesus (Asia) will swim in two seas...

and

The trembling of the earth at Mortara, the tin islands of St.George are half sunk...

The "tin islands of St. George" can be said to refer to the Scilly Islands, in St. George's Channel, off the coast of Cornwall in

*Left: The **Maharashtra earthquake** of 1993 occurred without warning and caused the death of more than 30,000 people. Doomsday interpreters believe that it heralds a series of super-quakes that will range across the world and culminate in its end.*

England, and this prediction has been interpreted to mean that the United Kingdom will suffer major earthquakes during the same period before the end of the millennium.

The Irish prophet St. Columba, who lived in the sixth century, predicted massive quakes would begin seven years before "Judgment Day", the year 2000, and Edgar Cayce, the famous American prophet and seer, stated that the British Isles and Western Europe would be altered by earthquakes and "inundations" in the "twinkling of an eye" towards the year 2000.

Once again, modern prophets of the twentieth century, such as Jeane Dixon, concur with Nostradamus's prophecy that the Earth at the beginning of the new millennium will shift its axis in two sudden jolts between the spring and fall of 2000.

There will be omens in the Spring, and extraordinary changes thereafter, reversals of Nations and mighty earthquakes...And there shall be in the month of October a great movement of the Globe, and it will be such that one will think the Earth has lost its natural gravitational movement and that it will be plunged into the abyss of perpetual darkness.

The concept of the Earth's axis shifting during the year 2000 is something that has been considered a possibility for many years. Evidence indicates that the polar ice-caps have moved from their present position at least two hundred times in the past billion years. These shifts are considered by many scientists to have been responsible for various prehistoric mass extinctions. Even human disasters in our distant past have been associated with such polar shifts. The sinking of Atlantis, for example, may have occurred at exactly the time of one of these shifts. In his book *Earth's Shifting Crust*, Charles Hapgood, Professor of Science at Keene College, New Hampshire, theorizes that polar shifts have happened three times in the past one hundred thousand years—that the north pole moved from its position in Canada's Yukon area to the sea of Greenland,

Above: *The southwest coast of England, showing the Scilly Isles (circled) and Cornwall as they appear now with the possible outline of the coast according to the prophecy.*

Opposite: *Ruins of the old tin mines of Cornwall which lie near the south-western tip of England. Nostradamus and others predicted that this part of England would be submerged beneath the sea.*

sliding back to the Hudson Bay and finally settling in its present place only twelve thousand years ago. This corresponds with Plato's dating of the sinking of Atlantis.

Hapgood suggests that polar shifts can happen because of alterations in the tides of molten lava caused by lateral rotation stresses, which he blames on the growth of Atlantic ice-caps. According to other modern writers such as the prophetic interpreter John Hogue, in his book *Nostradamus and the Millennium*, given the likelihood of an increasing wobble of the planet's rotation, we could see the lithosphere slide over the magnetic core.

On May 5, 2000, the new moon will align with Earth, the Sun, Jupiter, and Saturn, and five other planets will be pulling away from Earth on the other side of the Sun, creating a massive gravitational tug-o'-war, which may increase the already existing rotational "wobble" predicted for the earth at that time.

Writing in the science magazine *Nature*, the geophysicist Dr. R.Tomaschek suggested that during a study of 134 earthquakes with a measured magnitude of seven and three-quarters or more on the Richter scale, over a period of forty-three years, a significant number of the quakes occurred during times when Uranus was within fifteen degrees of its upper or lower transit of meridian of the epicenter of the quakes. Tomaschek believes, along with other scientists, that Uranus influenced at least three of this century's superquakes: the Tokyo quake of 1923, the Honshu quake of 1933, and the Assam quake in India during 1950. During May 5, 2000, Uranus may well create enough additional friction to influence the invisible gravity line of Saturn, Jupiter, the Sun and Moon, sufficient to cause the Earth to suffer massive superquakes across its surface and ultimately perhaps even shift it from its present polar axis.

*While the **Pyramid** (far left) and its enigmatic predictions remain hypothetical, the planetary line-up is very real. Along with the **Sun** (top) virtually all the planets are arrayed in a straight line , especially **Jupiter** (second from top), **Saturn** (third), and the **full moon** (bottom). The four images are not to scale.*

Future~Quakes
and Other Prophecies of
Edgar Cayce

EDGAR CAYCE, sometimes known as the "sleeping prophet," was born in Kentucky in 1877, and died in 1945, at the very end of World War II.

Cayce was given the name "the sleeping prophet" because of his ability to fall into deep trances during which he performed some of the most astounding feats of clairvoyance, healing, and prophecy. Even as a child he had already developed remarkable clairvoyant gifts, and as he grew up he continued to channel psychic information which he claimed was provided for humanity's betterment, in particular through healing others. He was not qualified in any way as a doctor, or formally in any other area of life, but in fact worked in a photographic shop in Virginia. During his life he healed and helped more than fifteen thousand individuals, by lying on a couch and falling into a trance during which the spirit world would give him information and advice on the needs of those that approached him.

Apart from his medical cures, he also, during these trances, spoke much about global issues. He prophesied, for example, that Russia would be "born again," and that Communism would end in the Soviet Union—a most successful prophecy. He also predicted that much of the new world order in religiousness and freedom would arise from the new Russia that would emerge, and that this would occur through an alliance with the United States of America. If we imagine that he saw this happening in the 1930s when there was

Above: ***Edgar Cayce.***
Opposite: ***Perestroika***—*the first crack. Cayce predicted the death of communism and the dissolution of the Soviet Union.*

absolutely no likelihood of such a result, we can see just how remarkable it was.

Cayce spoke also of China, and of how it would gradually change from an entrenched Communist country into a deeply Christian community with a democracy as powerful and fair as any other in the western civilized world. This, he predicted, would probably occur during the early few months of the twenty-first century, in the year 2000.

Cayce also had much to say about America in relation to Earth movements in the year 2000:

All over the country many physical changes of a minor or greater degree. The greater change will be in the North Atlantic Seaboard. Watch New York, Connecticut and the like.

Many portions of the East Coast will be disturbed, as well as many portions of the West Coast, as well as the central portion of the United States.

Portions of the now east coast of New York, or New York City itself, will in the main disappear. This will be another generation, though, here; while the southern portions of Carolina, Georgia, these will disappear. This will be much sooner.

The waters of the Great Lakes will empty into the Gulf of Mexico.

If there are greater activities in Vesuvius or Pelee, then the southern coast of California— and the areas between Salt Lake and the southern portions of Nevada—may expect, within three months following same, an inundation caused by earthquakes.

Safety lands will be the area around Norfolk, Virginia Beach, parts of Ohio, Indiana, and Illinois and much of the southern portion of Canada and the eastern portion of Canada.

The predicted new coastline of the USA *by the end of the year 2000. This model is based upon the fault lines, the present levels of the land above sea level, and the predictions of the various prophets.*

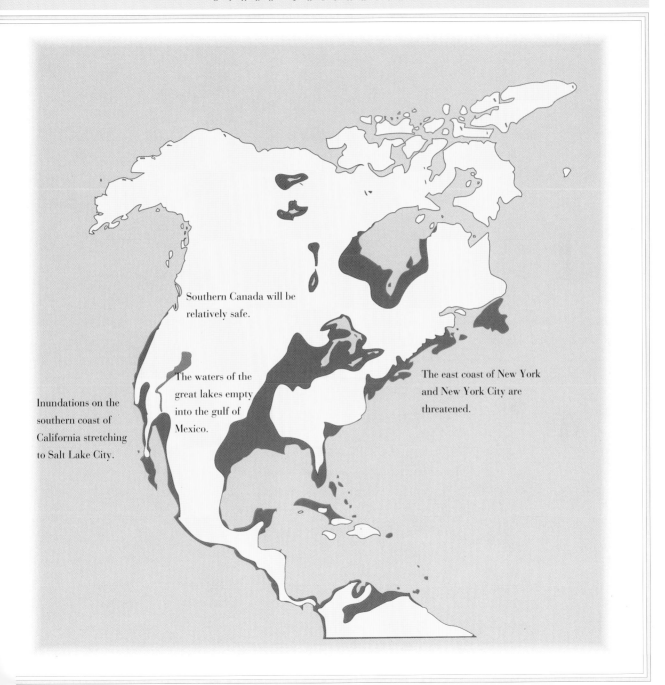

Southern Canada will be relatively safe.

Inundations on the southern coast of California stretching to Salt Lake City.

The waters of the great lakes empty into the gulf of Mexico.

The east coast of New York and New York City are threatened.

Cayce "saw" these activities in the physical state of America, during the same trances. He indicated that the shifting of the poles were a logical consequence of large-scale crustal displacements. Geologists have put such changes in a later period of our future, but Cayce insisted that they would occur during 2000 and 2001.

The processes will begin, Cayce says, with the changes in the South Pacific and Mediterranean, and the appearance of land near Bimini. The West Coast destruction will be early within these events, as will the inundations around Carolina and Georgia.

According to an article in *The Professional Geologist* published in 1966, since the time of Jesus Christ, two thousand years ago, some five million lives have been lost as a result of natural cataclysms, and a million of those, that is a fifth of the total, have been lost in the past one hundred years only. The author of the article, Bahngrell Brown, believes that the incidence of major earthquake activity is increasing rapidly during the latter years of the twentieth century, and that our only hope is to learn how to predict the quakes' occurrence so that areas imminently threatened may be evacuated to safer regions.

It may be noted that the spacing of these events over the last one hundred years would suggest that sacrifice in life is imminent. As we face the future, we might let our imaginations dwell on the likelihood of these long-overdue possibilities for that future:

1. A crater lake type eruption in the belt of the dormant US volcanoes.

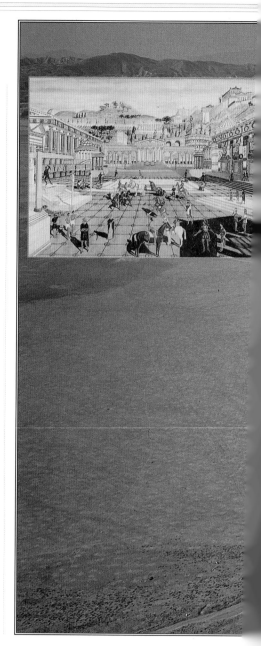

The San Andreas Fault. *Seismologists now suspect areas to the north of the fault were responsible for the recent quakes.*

Inset: *The fabled lost land of **Atlantis**, which supposedly sank when the Earth shifted its axis twelve thousand years ago.*

2. A recurrence of the terrible 1811-12 earthquake in the Mississippi Valley, where there are now great cities.

3. Any mountain city in an avalanche path.

The most dramatic earthquake potential in the United States is still that which centers on the Californian San Andreas Fault. A trench six hundred miles long runs along the coast of California, with many branches cutting into wider areas to the east. The quakes of 1838, 1906, and 1957 were the largest to occur in the US during recent history, but the rumblings of the San Andreas Fault were "audible" during that period, somehow giving geologists the sense that quakes would not be too massive. In recent years, during the latter part of the twentieth century, the fault has gone suspiciously silent, and scientists are concerned that it may be building up to a gigantic quake—the so-called "Big One"—which has been expected for some time now.

Numerous predictions have been made by many of the better-known prophets, and interpreted during this century in attempts to point to actual likely dates. Very few of them have been successful. May of 1993 was a favorite date. In the case of one prediction (made by V.J. Hewitt interpreting Nostradamus), a date and even a time were given for the start of an eleven-minute quake that would level much of the West Coast including Hollywood and the movie studios. But this did not occur and only a relatively minor quake at the beginning of 1994 damaged a small area and killed some forty people. Though hardly to be diminished in its tragic effects, that quake was not on the scale of the one in Maharashtra, India, during late September 1993, where there was a death-toll of thirty thousand people.

Given that Cayce was so successful in many of his prophecies

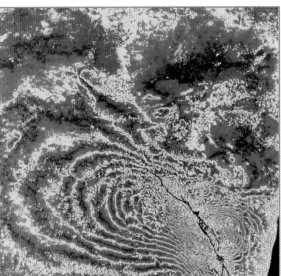

regarding the United States, we might take some interest in predictions he made in relation to civil unrest during the last years of the twentieth century and the first years of the twenty-first.

Cayce foresaw race riots:

Though there may come those periods when there will be great stress, as brother rises against brother, as group or sect or race rises against race—yet the levelling must come.

He also predicted a full-scale revolution within the United States because of the social gap between the rich and poor:

Those in position (must) give of their means, their wealth, their education, their position.

For unless these are considered, there must eventually become a revolution in this country—and there will be a dividing of the sections as one against another. For these are the levelling means and manners to which men resort when there is the plenty in some areas and a lack of sustenance in the life of others.

Above left: **Computer model predictions** *of the ground movements around the San Andreas Fault were found to be remarkably accurate when compared with images taken from the* **ERS-1 satellite** *(above right).*

Jeane Dixon ~ Living Prophet

Almost all of our greatest and most successful prophets have long been dead. Their legacies are still much referred to in many cases, such as that of Nostradamus, whose works have never been out of print in the four hundred years since his death. Much of what these "old" prophets say is too general to apply to ordinary events taking place in our lives, or events that are likely to take place in the year 2000. But Jeane Dixon is very much alive today, and still making predictions from her home in the United States.

A gentle but strong woman in the later years of her life (she does not reveal her age), Jeane Dixon believes her powers to be God-given, and still attends daily mass in her local town. She has gained an extraordinary reputation due to some dramatic successes, including prophecies related to history-making events such as the assassinations of both John and Robert Kennedy, and the disastrous explosion of the Apollo space capsule at Cape Kennedy in 1967. She has also shown an ability to predict smaller events, even related to her husband and friends in her local neighborhood. Within the United States she has become a legend in her own lifetime.

There are numerous events which Ms Dixon has singled out for the years 1999 and 2000 and beyond, which have much in common with the predictions of famous prophets of our past. She states categorically that in 1999, for example, the process of disarmament that by then will have continued for several decades, will be proven false, and a third world war will break out. If we remember,

Above: *Jeane Dixon*, *the best-known living prophet of the twentieth century.*
Opposite: *Astronauts Virgil Grissom, Edward White and Roger Chaffee before the ill fated Apollo One disaster at Cape Kennedy, in which all three died. This was one of her most famous prophecies.*

Nostradamus named the year 1999 as one in which major changes would occur in the US, related to a powerful religious figure who would appear in New York on Manhattan Island. Ms Dixon agrees with this insofar as she refers to an "antichrist," whom she says is already alive today in the Middle East. Nostradamus also placed what he called "the third Antichrist" (he predicted Napoleon and Hitler as the first and second) in the Middle East.

Jeane Dixon describes this individual as one who will imitate Christ's lifestyle and religious philosophy, becoming enormously popular through an expression of love for all humanity, and disguising his true intentions, which Ms Dixon predicts will be satanic in origin. The United States will provide massive propaganda to glorify his name and promote his position as a world leader. Many

Manhattan Island, New York.

Supposedly a powerful religious figure will appear connected to Manhattan Island. One of Dixon's most dramatic prophecies mirrors that of Nostradamus. She tells of an "anti-Christ" who will seduce the United States into behavior which will result in a disadvantage to the nation and the world. This individual is already living in the Middle East and will emerge and gain masses of disciples through his ability to inspire love and loyalty.

Hillary Clinton, *predicted by some to be the first female president of the United States by the year 2000 or 2004.*

young people will become his disciples, taken in by his charm and charisma. Jeane Dixon writes:

The Antichrist will be a phenomenon of the political order. He is not simply a religious "heretic" whom the world at large could simply ignore. No! He will hold earthly power in his hands and use it as his instrument. All the tyrants in history are mere children in comparison with him.

This means first of all that he will be a military figure beyond anything the world has previously seen. He will conquer the whole earth and hold it in complete mastery with the most modern weapons. He will rule his new World Empire with the utmost of military might and glory.

Ms Dixon believes that this Antichrist to beat all Antichrists will only be defeated by the arrival of the Messiah, by the Second Coming of Christ, and that humanity will witness "the shadow of the cross, the tremor of the earth and three days of darkness" before the Messiah arrives to save us all from destruction through the third world war at the end of the century.

Much of this prophetic material is echoed in both the Bible, particularly in the Book of Revelation as we have seen, and in the prophecies of Nostradamus and others of our past. The concept that the world is passing through the pre-Last Judgment scenario during the final years of the 1990s is a powerful one, and Ms Dixon seems very much to have linked into this, perhaps through her strong ties

Dixon believes that we shall find intelligent life quite close to our own world, and that we shall journey there, finally to understand that mankind is not original to Earth—the last of the great human race-ego-trips.

to the Christian Church, and her powerful belief in God's gift of prophecy to her.

Her prophecies range across many other, equally dramatic subjects, such as the discovery of intelligent life on a sister "planet exactly on the other side of the sun", which humanity will discover by means of powerful instruments placed on Jupiter which will give us "a bird's eye view" of these alien peoples. She predicted unsuccessfully that the first woman US president would be elected in the 1980s, while others pitch the date to be the year 2000, and Hillary Clinton. She tells us that the world will not come to an end for at least another 3000 years, while Nostradamus predicted the end of the world to be in the mid-3000s. By the century's end, we are promised that Canada and Brazil will be amongst the world's most powerful nations because of their growing resources.

Peace in Northern Ireland was supposed, according to Ms Dixon, to occur in 1988, whereas it seems to be occurring in the 1990s, and by the end of the century, according to Ms Dixon, in the year 2000, almost all world famine will be at an end.

Her predictions are brave, with precise dates in many cases—far braver than most other prophets, who had a habit of avoiding any kind of precision, perhaps because of the restrictions of heretical laws up to the Middle Ages. The result is that she is often wrong, but when she is right, there is no doubt that the events predicted by her are sufficient to make us forget the mistakes.

The Sibylline Oracles

During the latter years of the Roman Empire, the Sibylline Oracles gave some relief to the rest of the disastrous prophecies that beset those times. The Oracles were originally fictional Greek writings which were intended to convert pagan peoples to Judaism, and the Christians of Roman times used them in adapted versions to attempt the same task, to convert the people of their times to the new Christianity.

The idea was that the hero of the Oracles was the risen Christ who appears in the Book of Revelation, who fights the good fight against the antichrist. This antichrist has been, in turn, and according to prophets of our past, various Roman Emperors, particularly Nero, who was very unpopular with the early Christians, Napoleon, Hitler and others.

As we are expecting, according to numerous ancient and modern seers, another antichrist in the next few years, it might be well to chant one of the best and most lyrical Sibylline Oracles again today. In their book *Prophecies of the Presidents—The Spiritual Destiny of America Revealed*, Timothy Green Beckley and Arthur Crockett suggest that the following Sibylline Oracle describes the future world peace that the United States will achieve in the year 2000 and thereafter.

The Kingdom of God shall come upon all good men; for Earth, which is the produce of all things, shall yield to men the best, and infinite fruits. And the Cities shall be full of good men, and the fields shall be fruitful, and there shall be no war upon the Earth, nor tumult, nor shall the Earth groan as by an earthquake. No wars,

Opposite: ***The Last Judgement***, *by William Blake. According to most Christian representations of the end, there follows quite smartly another beginning—better, of course, than the present.*

no drought, nor famine, nor hail to waste the fruits... for there shall be no more wars.

No wars, no drought, nor famine, nor hail to waste the fruits; but there shall be great peace in all the Earth, and one King shall live in friendship with the other to the end of the age.

And the immortal, who lives in the heavens adorned with stars, shall give common law to all men in all of the Earth, and instruct miserable men that things must be done; for he is the only God, and there is no other. And he shall burn the great strength of men by Fire.

Then he shall raise a Kingdom forever over all men when he hath given a Holy Law to the Righteous, to all whom he promised to open the Earth; and the world of the blessed, and all joys, and an immortal mind, and eternal cheerfulness. Out of every country they shall bring Frankincense, and gifts to the houses of the Great God, and there shall be no other house to be enquired for by the generations of men that are to come, but the faithful Man whom God has given to be worshipped, for mortals call him the Son of the Great God.

And all paths of the fields, and rough shores, and high mountains, and the raging waves of the sea, shall be easily passed or sailed through in those days; for all peace shall happen to the good, through all their land, the Prophets of the Great God shall take away all slaughter... for they are the judges of mortals...and the righteous Kings. And there shall be just riches for men, for the government of the Great God shall be just judgment.

Now no longer shall gold and silver be full of guile, nor shall there be possessing of land nor toilsome slavery; but one love and one ordering of life in kindness of soul. All things shall be common and light equal in the lives of men.

Vice shall leave the earth and be sunk in the divine ocean. Then this is the summer of mortal men nigh at hand. Strong necessity will be laid upon the world that these things be accomplished. No wayfarer meeting another will then say: "The race of mortal men, though now they perish, shall some day have rest."

And then a holy people shall wield the sceptre of the whole world through all the ages, along with their mighty offspring.

The Future of God

*In the final persecution of the Holy Roman Church there will reign
Peter the Roman, who will feed his flock among many tribulations;
after which the seven-hilled city will be destroyed and the dreadful Judge will judge the people.* MALACHY

Almost all of the major prophets in our past, such as Nostradamus,
Cayce, Malachy, and St. John, had something to say about the
established Church of Christianity, and in particular about the
Catholic leaders—the Popes, and the changes that will come around
the year 2000 in the Catholic Church.

The Irish prophet Malachy O'Morgair, who lived in the eleventh
century, offered some astounding predictions related to each of the
popes that followed his life. Malachy was considered to be a divine
prophet during his life and is believed to have performed miracles,
healing the sick, and levitating. Upon his death in 1184, while
visiting France, he left a series of written statements related to the
identity of all the popes right up to our own time, and including John
Paul II—Karol Wojtyla—and three more popes who come to the
throne of the Vatican thereafter.

The descriptions of earlier popes are remarkable and apt in each
case. For example he called Pope Alexander IV, who was previously
Cardinal of Ostia, "Signum Ostiensis", and Pope Paul VI, who used
a coat of arms in the design of the *fleur de lys*, was called "Flors
Florum", or "flower of flowers." John Paul I, who remained pope for

Above: ***The Vatican City flag.***
Opposite: *The birth of patriarchal
society.* **God surrounded by His angels,**
*a fifteenth-century Italian
representation of God as a benevolent
and powerful father-figure.*

only thirty-three days. was named "The Half Moon." and John Paul
II became "The Sun's Labor" implying a pope who has to struggle
with a waning Catholicism.

The last two popes in Malachy's list are "Gloriae Olivae" and
"Petrus Romanus"—Peter of Rome. Given the usual age of Catholic
popes, the implication is that the last two popes will live around the
end of this century and that the Catholic Church and its connection
with the papacy will end around the year 2000.

Papal Consecration of 1988 in St. Peters, Rome.

Nostradamus also had much to say about the last days of the Catholic Church coming towards the end of the twentieth century. One of his most famous verses actually dates the culmination as occurring in July 1999 when a major religious event will take place on the island of Manhattan.

The year 1999 and seven months, from the skies will come a great and frightening King, to resuscitate the great King of Angouleme, before [and] after Mars to reign through happiness.

The verse refers to the "King of Angouleme," a clever metaphor for Manhattan Island, derived from the island's previous name, Angouleme, named by its first discoverer, Giovanni da Verrazano (of Verrazano Bridge fame), whose master was King Francis I of France, also named Count Angouleme. The link between this verse and the fall of Catholicism at the end of this century is made finally by the fact that Francis I's (King of Angouleme) name is used in the lines. Francis spent twenty-three years of his reign battling with the Holy Roman Empire.

We are told also in another verse that John Paul II will die in 1996 and that during the following papal election—the election that will result in the pope that Malachy called "Gloriae Olivae"— there will be two main contenders for the papacy, one Spanish, the other French. And the French pope will be elected. Will this next pope be French, and will his name or his past have some connection with olives? And the final pope—"Petrus Romanus"—will he actually be the very last in the long line of the papacy to grace the throne of the Vatican?

How Many Humans?

WORLD POPULATION PROJECTIONS

YEAR	POPULATION
1985	5,333,000,000
2000	6,240,000,000
2010	7,250,000,000
2015	8,850,000,000
2020	10,800,000,000

P robably the most significant single factor in the way the future will develop lies in the number of us that collect on this planet during the next decade. This will affect almost every aspect of life on earth, from communication to all forms of social interaction.

At the end of 1993 the *Encyclopaedia Britannica* recorded world population to have reached 5,436,358,000 people—that is on average 103.7 people for every square mile of land. The projection of population growth between that time and the year 2010 is that a further 1,813,642,000 more people will be born and survive than will die. That gives us a total of 7,250,000,000 by that date. Working backwards, we come to a number for the beginning of the year 2000—6,240,000,000.

This is on the conservative side, and based on demographic growth over the years before 1993. But there are other statistical expectations of a much higher growth rate.

To give us a little perspective we can look briefly back into our past. In 1825, when population growth had become a precise field of study due to the work of Thomas Robert Malthus, who in 1798 compiled a study of the subject entitled *Essay on the Principle of Population*, there were around a billion people on Earth. It had taken thousands of years to reach that number. By then, improvements in medical care and the increase of industrialization were causing the population to accelerate

WORLD'S MOST POPULOUS NATIONS

1985	2020
1 China	1 India
2 India	2 China
3 Soviet Union	3 Nigeria
4 United States	4 Pakistan
5 Japan	5 Russian States
6 Indonesia	6 Brazil
7 Brazil	7 Indonesia
8 United Kingdom	8 United States
9 Germany	9 Bangladesh
10 Italy	10 Iran
11 Bangladesh	11 Ethiopia
12 France	12 Philippines
13 Nigeria	13 Mexico
14 Pakistan	14 Vietnam
15 Mexico	15 Kenia
16 Spain	16 Zaire
17 Vietnam	17 Egypt
18 Poland	18 Tanzania
19 Egypt	19 Turkey
20 Philippines	20 Japan
21 Turkey	21 Saudi Arabia
22 South Korea	22 Thailand
23 Ethiopia	23 Uganda
24 Thailand	24 Sudan

* Developing countries in red

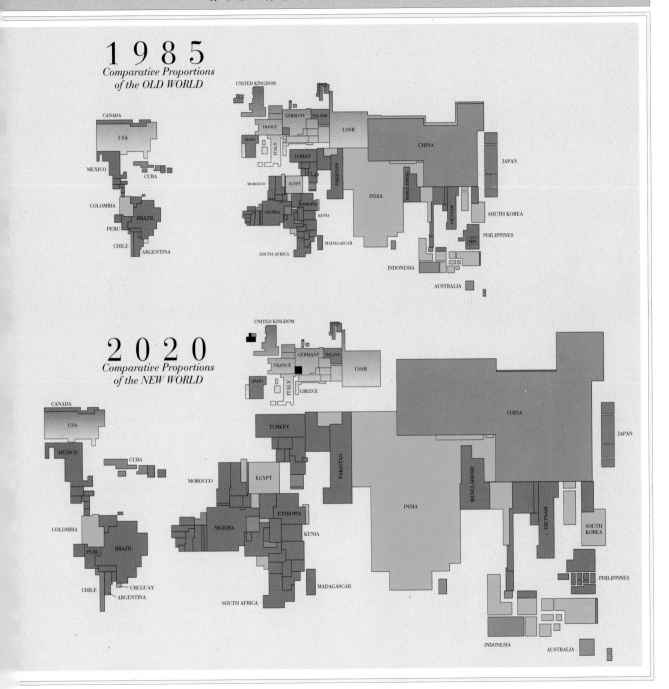

1985
*Comparative Proportions
of the OLD WORLD*

2020
*Comparative Proportions
of the NEW WORLD*

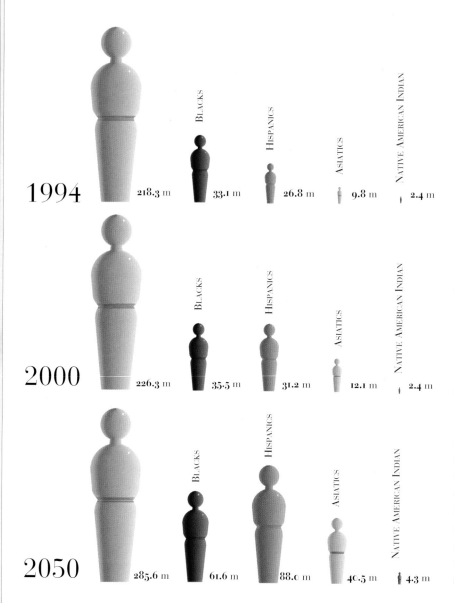

1994

218.3 m — BLACKS 33.1 m — HISPANICS 26.8 m — ASIATICS 9.8 m — NATIVE AMERICAN INDIAN 2.4 m

2000

226.3 m — BLACKS 35.5 m — HISPANICS 31.2 m — ASIATICS 12.1 m — NATIVE AMERICAN INDIAN 2.4 m

2050

285.6 m — BLACKS 61.6 m — HISPANICS 88.0 m — ASIATICS 40.5 m — NATIVE AMERICAN INDIAN 4.3 m

As can be seen in these projections, based upon figures compiled by the Bureau of Census, the numerical supremacy of White America will be seriously challenged by the year 2000. Within twenty years the multi-racial group of Hispanics will be more numerous than American blacks and within a few decades Asians will have almost equalled the size of the black communities. What this will mean in terms of inter-racial tensions is hard to imagine, and yet the future holds great promise that America will be the first truly multi-racial nation and culture representing the various races of the Earth under one federation.

The Year 2050

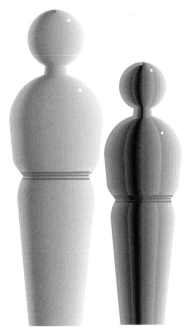

Whites
285.6 m

Combined Races
194.4 m

America's population growth will far outstrip the growth rates of other industrialized nations. But this growth will be mainly in the American Hispanic communities which could triple within the next five decades. By the mid twenty-first century whites will almost be overtaken by the combination of all other races, which could completely change American culture.

and in the next one hundred years the figure doubled to two billion, and then doubled again in the following fifty years, reaching four billion by 1976.

Since 1990, the rate of growth has slowed down slightly because of a reduction in fertility rates in the western civilized world, but it will be a very long time before we feel the effect of this. In fact there will not be a levelling of human population growth, to the point where only the same number of people are born as die, before the middle of the twenty-first century. By that time there could be around fifteen billion people elbowing for space on planet Earth.

The growth of population will not, of course, occur evenly across the whole planet. Some groups will grow faster than others. Taking as an example the United States—a country with a wide cross-section of different races—during 1994 there were approximately 218.3 million whites in the country, 33.1 million blacks, 26.8 million Hispanics, 9.8 million Asians, and 2.4 million Native Americans.

By the year 2000 it is estimated that there will be 226.3 million whites (an increase of 3.6%), 35.5 million blacks (an increase of 7.2%), 31.2 millions Hispanics (an increase of 16%), 12.1 million Asians (an increase of 23%), and that the Native American population will remain stable. From then to the year 2050, an even bigger jump will take place with increases of whites by only a further 26%, while blacks will increase by 73%, Hispanics 182%, Asians 234%, and Native Americans almost 100%. By halfway through the twenty-first century, therefore, there will be almost as many non-whites in the United States as whites. This will also be reflected in other parts of the world, particularly with the growth of population numbers in countries such as China and India.

Citification

Another of the most rapid growth patterns that will become still more evident during the year 2000 is the move of populations to and from cities. More and more people in the developing world are rushing to live in urban areas while the wealthy in the rich world are running away from them. For those who currently dwell in, or commute to, the major cities of the world, the experiences of traffic jams, crime, over-population, car-parking problems and general stress are entirely familiar. Each year it becomes more and more difficult to reach offices or homes with the number of vehicles growing already out of control. During the mid-1990s we have seen a much greater interest in books and information, television and cinema concerned with silence and solitude - places to retreat to, music that brings tranquillity, vacations "away from it all." This is a natural response to the greater instance of overcrowding in cities. But the trend during the last years of the millennium will increase city populations still further.

To give some perspective we can look at city population numbers during, for example, the 1950s. The biggest city in the world then was New York, with approximately 12.3 million inhabitants. London came second with 8.7 million. Tokyo had 6.9 million people walking its streets, while Paris, Moscow and Buenos Aires enjoyed around 5 million each. By 1990 New York was way outnumbered by Tokyo which contained 25 million people! That's an increase of almost three times. New York in 1990 was at 16 million, London left behind at less than 10 million, while Mexico City had grown to 15 million, and Buenos Aires tipped 11.4 million.

The estimates for the year 2010 are that Tokyo will hit 29 million,

Opposite: **The Twin Petronas Towers** *in Kuala Lumpur, due to be completed in 1996, will finally exceed the height of the Sears Tower in Chigaco. Such monumental structures as this Malaysian tower symbolize the growing affluence of the nations around the Pacific rim and their determination to become leading industrial powers in the world in the next century.*

NEW YORK

MEXICO CITY

BOMBAY

TOKYO

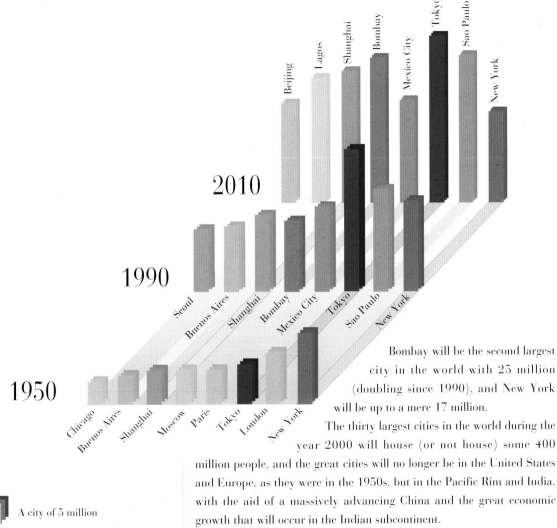

2010

1990

1950

Beijing
Lagos
Shanghai
Bombay
Mexico City
Tokyo
Sao Paulo
New York

Seoul
Buenos Aires
Shanghai
Bombay
Mexico City
Tokyo
Sao Paulo
New York

Chicago
Buenos Aires
Shanghai
Moscow
Paris
Tokyo
London
New York

A city of 5 million

The diagram above illustrates the massive growth of cities in the developing world. It would seem that in the richer and more established world the cities are shrinking, New York and Tokyo being the exceptions.

Bombay will be the second largest city in the world with 25 million (doubling since 1990), and New York will be up to a mere 17 million.

The thirty largest cities in the world during the year 2000 will house (or not house) some 400 million people, and the great cities will no longer be in the United States and Europe, as they were in the 1950s, but in the Pacific Rim and India, with the aid of a massively advancing China and the great economic growth that will occur in the Indian subcontinent.

The by-product of this lemming-like rush for city areas will be the rush away from them by those who are currently beginning to become overwhelmed by the increasing numbers, noise, crime and general threat of the city. By the early years of the next millennium it is likely that England, for example, will be one massive suburb!

Economic Apocalypse

According to most political economic forecasters, the ones we hear most often, the future looks rosier than the past. Western society has recently, in the first few years of the 1990s, passed through a major recession and come out the other side. Life will improve, they tell us.

But there are two forecasters, working together as one, who have a completely different, and totally disastrous series of prophecies for the financial year 2000.

In their book *The Great Reckoning*, James Dale Davidson and William Rees-Mogg paint a picture of the likely economic future we shall face in the first year of the twenty-first century. And reading it tends to make one wish to run to the bank, draw out all the savings and hide them away under the mattress!

Briefly, they state that since World War Two, Western society has undergone a long-term credit expansion and economic boom which must now reach, in fact already is reaching, a conclusion. Matters like the fall of the Berlin Wall, the end of the Cold War, and the collapse of Communism must give birth to a new world order, or rather, disorder. This kind of change must inevitably, they state, result in crises, because our fundamental methods of trading and funding global cash flow and profit and loss now has no solid base. During the early 1990s the major economies of the world, such as the United States, Japan and Europe, were increasingly supported by the interest due on vast debts owed both within countries and across various borders, making the wealth and prosperity of these larger countries increasingly dependent on those that had borrowed the money: institutions, organizations and countries that

In only a decade and a half America's gross federal debt will increase by almost 450%, to a massive 6,831 billion dollars. There is simply no way this can ever be repaid as the total income of the nation hardly even pays the interest upon such a sum. By the year 2000 drastic measures will have to be taken by the government through either the inflation or deflation of the currency. Either way this could prove disastrous for America.

1984

$1,557 bn

Gross federal debt 1984, 1994 and
projections for the year 2000.

1994

2000

$4,770 bn

$6,831bn

were, as it became evident, too weak to meet their obligations. Very often, they point out, the weakest debtors proved also to be the biggest, even within, for example, the United States itself—organizations such as savings and loans companies, insurance companies, banks and even the government itself. Many of these borrowers, if looked at closely, were actually already insolvent, and being propped up in order not to set off a kind of multiple collapse, like a house of cards.

The 1980s had created what the authors call "a generation of budget deficits without tears", providing false confidence, while the unpaid bills, the debts, nevertheless continued to compound interest.

By the year 1992, the gross interest on the national debt of the United States was accounting for 62% of federal income tax collected.

Davidson and Rees-Mogg estimate that in the same year the foreign indebtedness of the United States was around $850 billion, which was about double the total US exports for the same year. This kind of ratio—debt to export, running at 200%—is unusually high even for a Third World country.

Put another way, consider the situation on the level of your own personal income and borrowing. You have an annual income of, say, $50,000, and a bank loan of $100,000. If you do not service that debt, at least to keep the interest paid, it will compound at a very rapid rate and pretty soon the capital owed and the increased interest each year will be too high to be serviced out of so small an income.

According to the predictions in the book, the interest payments due on American loans would be as much as the total Gross

The Diagram below illustrates the relationship of the total US exports against the total foreign debt incurred by the United States. This figure was $850 billion in 1992 while exports only yeilded half that amount. The lengthening shadow of debt coulds bring about a financial Armagedon by the year 2000.

Foreign debts incurred by the USA in 1992.

Total US Exports in 1992.

1992

National Product by the year 2015—i.e. all the US income earned during the year would be needed just to pay the interest on the debts, without touching the capital. Of course, this will not be allowed to happen, and by around 2000 the debt will have to be wiped out, either through economic deflationary measures which would inevitably cause a complete collapse of the US economy, or through inflation which will destroy the value and power of the US dollar.

The result of such scenarios by the end of the millennium would probably be hundreds of thousands of bankruptcies across the US, both in private businesses, public businesses and welfare state, thereby causing breakdown of authority and ultimately, the authors tell us, the very real threat of physical violence on a scale never before imagined. They call the up-coming change "The Great Reckoning," and recommend that we all prepare for it now. For it is the beginning of the end of the American "Empire," an ending that has been mirrored throughout history in other collapses—Ancient Rome, the Austro-Hungarian Empire, the British Empire—except that in this case much of the world is greatly dependent upon the American "Empire." All this fits very well with the predictions of Jeane Dixon and Edgar Cayce, providing an economic basis for the national civil unrest that they tell us will occur.

Total capital owed by USA.

Interest due on American loans.

Total US Gross National Product.

2015

Woman~Power

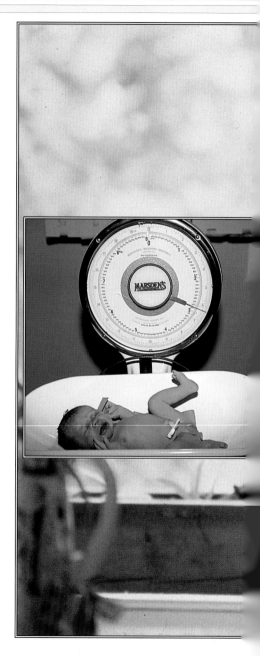

According to many prophecies from a variety of sources one of the biggest features of the beginning of the twenty-first century will be the increasing influence of feminine energy on human society. Women will continue to make their mark on industry, law, government, and religion in ever increasing numbers. This will do, of course, much for those institutions that have been dominated by male energy for so many centuries, very often to their disadvantage. But this situation does not simply arise from the dominance of the male spirit, though this is a large part of the problem. It also arises because of a predominantly aggressive society—our society, and its ability to indoctrinate newborn babies. Anthropological research has shown that in aggressive societies such as ours in the western world during the twentieth century, the baby is removed from the mother into the hands of hospital staff as early after birth as possible so as to begin the process of social indoctrination. A clinical attitude is quickly imposed upon the child by the nurses and doctors, under the guise of health and efficiency. This early "aura" surrounding the child's highly receptive and sensitive body and mind, presents the social environment, lacking intimacy and love. A fresh and innocent child is quickly taught the processes of an angry society and another aggressive individual is thereby launched onto the world.

According to Patricia Aburdene and John Naisbitt in their book

The image of the female most favored by male dominated societies, seems to be a kind of sex kitten, or an essentially docile child bearer. But the kitten has recently turned into a cat which appears to follow its own path, irrespective of the traditional values. Inset: As women re-evaluate their role as mothers, the aggressive male routines surrounding birth, midwifery, and baby care are revealed to be a brutal entry into what we increasingly find as a violent society.

Margaret Thatcher, *Prime Minister , U.K.*

Tansu Cilla, *Prime Minister, Turkey.*

Mary Robinson, *President, Republic of Ireland.*

Kim Campbell, *Prime Minister, Canada.*

Benazir Bhutto, *President, Pakistan.*

Golda Meir, *Prime Minister, Israel.*

Indira Gandhi, *Prime Minister, India.*

Corazon Aquino, *President of the Phillipines.*

As women achieve greater power in greater numbers, perhaps the world will grow softer, stronger, and less warlike, or perhaps women will simply make the same mistakes as men.

Megatrends for Women, men have maintained control over women by numerous subtle, and not so subtle means. For example, the use of the epidural lumbar puncture and other pain-killing drugs, employed ostensibly to reduce the discomfort of birth, actually succeed in disempowering the woman and empowering the doctor/society instead.

With a greater balance of women in positions of power, the very foundation of human society will change for the better, perhaps eventually giving a new energy that will allow western society to cease its everlasting conflicts. New methods of childbirth influenced by the greater power of femininity will influence the future and reduce the instance of aggression in the social arena. This may be the beginning of Nostradamus's and St. John the Divine's prophecies of a thousand years of peace in the next millennium.

In any event, women will, it is predicted by Aburdene and Naisbitt, have a greatly enhanced power position in society as a whole. This will not simply be a minor shift in attitudes but a mega-change that will touch almost all aspects of society. The family, for example, which we might call the security factor in life—the spiritual equivalent of the atom—is likely to undergo further breakdown. The father will cease to be the patriarchal figure he has been for hundreds, even thousands of years. Marriage and monogamy are already less than reliable staples of social order, and pretty soon we won't even be able to rely upon religion as a fall-back. Relationships will alter across all aspects of social interaction—between man and woman, parent and child, priest and faithful. And more than any other single "unit" of life women will be the source of these changes. More has happened to alter the role of women in society in the past thirty years or so than in two millennia before that, and yet true feminine equality still hasn't emerged completely, though it will by the beginning of the twenty-first century. This paradigm change will be both greatly challenging and exciting, and deeply unsettling. Authority in the world of industry, law, academia, medicine, politics will feel displaced as more and more women come into these spheres.

Not only do the statisticians and modern prophets confirm this trend, but we are told of a growth in female influence even by the prophets of the past. Nostradamus wrote of the end of the twentieth century being a time for the enrichment of the world by women:

With a name so wild will she be brought forth
That the three sisters will have the name for destiny:
Then she will lead a great people by tongue and deed,
More than any other will she have fame and renown.
CENTURY 1: 76

The first and most obvious areas that feel the impact of women are those of state and church, and we find that Nostradamus had things to

Opposite: *Perhaps the greatest woman leader of this century, **Indira Gandhi**, Prime Minister of India, had a deeply spiritual side to her nature, as well as a shrewd and often ruthless political mind. But such a blatant display of female power in a predominantly male society inevitably provokes the assassin.*

Hillary and Bill Clinton *at an*
inaugural dinner in Washington. Will
the most powerful woman in the world
become the most powerful person in the
world?

say about the growing presence of women such as Margaret Thatcher
and Hillary Clinton in positions of governmental power, and the female
place in the established Churches. Nostradamus tells us that women will
not only appear increasingly within the Protestant Christian Church, but
eventually also in the Catholic Church, forming a major influence in the
changes that will occur during the early years of the twenty-first century.

One of the single most significant events that would reflect the greater
influence of women would be the election of the first female president of
the United States, which could well occur in the year 2000. There are
those who suggest that this could be Hillary Clinton herself.

Owing to disappointments that will have occurred in previous
presidential terms, the world will perhaps be ready for a big change.

Great developments will occur also in industry and all areas of the
business world. According to *Megatrend*, during 1977 there were only
two million female-owned businesses in the US, turning over revenues of
$25 billion. By 1988 there were five million female-owned businesses
with revenues of over $83 billion. During that eleven-year period,
independent businesses overall increased revenues by some 56%, while
female businesses increased by over 129%. According to the old and new
prophets, this trend continues and increases in a giant exponential curve
towards the end of the millennium, contributing enormously to the
general critical mass.

Family Futures

One of the developments of society that is predicted by the writer and forecaster Alvin Toffler in his book *Future Shock* may result from the increased presence of feminine power, is a new way of gathering together in family groups.

The family—the "shock absorber" of society, Toffler tells us—has long been the haven to which the beaten individual returns after doing battle with the world. Working people, children at school, drivers in traffic jams, etc., all come home after a weary day and collapse into the family unit, where they can recharge their batteries and hopefully return to the fray once more the following morning.

But as the future unfolds new areas of stress, new religions, new attitudes to sex, and relationships, this shock absorber, Toffler tells us, will have to navigate larger and larger bumps in the road.

Already in the last years of the twentieth century the family is showing itself to be a harbor of discontent in ways that would never have been admitted in the earlier years of the century. Sexual deviations, criminal inclinations, anxiety dominations, and childcare abominations are all players in the arena of the nuclear family fallout. Is it that we in the late twentieth century have invented such behavior, or that it was always there and only now becomes publicly shared?

Mr. and Mrs. Terry of London with some of their nineteen children, 1914. Such a scene could equally have come from any of the industrial nations, which saw the big family as the bricks and mortar of society. Since those days the family unit has been rapidly shrinking, its members becoming more isolated, more privileged but at the same time more lonely.

Desert well, *Sahel, Mali. Perhaps one day we shall overcome our need for mass gathering in vast areas called cities, and return to the old tribal concept of the commune. This might then be called a real "Commune-ism."*

On the other hand perhaps this is merely a transition period during which we are finding new family feet, new ways of co-existing that will result in a golden age of the family. Perhaps the increasing turbulence of life will give rise to a deeper entrenchment of family values, and perhaps people will marry more successfully in order to establish stability for themselves and an anchor against the storms of the rest of the world. Or perhaps a third possibility—a new kind of family altogether.

The predictions we have already seen in this book—a new kind of feminine presence, more people on the planet, a greater instance of peace, new ways to bring children closer to the mother's breast, different ways to relate to one another more freely—according to Toffler all add up to a more extended family unit.

As rapid change increases the loneliness and alienation in society, we may look forward to group marriages and larger families made up of several adults gathering together against the problems of isolation. In *Future Shock* Alvin Toffler suggests that experiments in the 1960s may become more common by the year 2000. "Corporate families" will form in which perhaps as many as six adults will adopt a single name, living and raising children together, and gaining economic and tax advantages from the arrangement.

Certainly, during the last years of the 1990s there are already plenty

Sheep herding, *Sierra, California. Are we being driven like sheep towards the new millennium, or shall we finally take responsibility for our new lives and our own, precious world?*

of examples of group families and communes, such as the experiments being undertaken in the Findhorn Foundation and the Buddhist commune, Samye Ling, both in Scotland. Ranging from small, extended families to fully fledged communes, such as the Osho Commune in India, where there are several thousand members and completely different attitudes to living together in harmony, the way is set for a very different future.

Toffler tells us that communalism began in those parts of society which lay outside the standard money earning sectors, such as retired people, drop-outs, students, and the spiritual minorities. But as time goes on and into the next century, according to Toffler, the experiments will be seen to have worked successfully and the extended family and commune will open into broader sectors. With the increase of technologies which allow us to work at home, such as computer systems with on-line capabilities, it will become possible for larger numbers of people to live without commuting to offices every day, thereby giving a greater freedom to choose their living and working environments. Also, as relationships generally become more easily polygamous—in other words moral attitudes become more liberal and what is already happening in secret can happen openly—so communal living will be more attractive to a greater number of people.

THE BIBLIOGRAPHY

History is full of prophets. We have discovered just a few of them in the pages of this book, but there are literally thousands more in our past who have written, often at length, about our future. The following are a further sample of these, and the books that have been associated with them. We start with the few most famous, and then the rest are given in alphabetical order.

NOSTRADAMUS

The original work of Michel de Nostradame was entitled *The Centuries*. This consisted of ten volumes of his obscurely written prophecies in verse form, with just short of 1000 verses. These are currently published in various editions with commentaries by a number of modern interpreters such as Erika Cheetham, and Henry C. Roberts. Nostradamus' verses are very difficult to understand and even more difficult to interpret as "sensible" prophecies relating to our future. The best currently published volumes are as follows:

Michel de Nostradame

Leoni, Edgar. *Nostradamus and His Prophecies*, New York, Bell.

This is probably the best of all of the interpretations and the one that forms the basis for most modern interpreters.

Edgar Cayce

Cheetham, Erika. *The Prophecies of Nostradamus*. Various paperback editions. The author's own translation, selection and interpretation.

Roberts, Henry C. *The Complete Prophecies of Nostradamus*. Various paperback editions. The author's own translation, selection and interpretation.

Hogue, John. *Nostradamus and the Millennium*, New York: Doubleday Books 1987. The first of the illustrated interpretations of the prophecies.

Lorie, Peter. *Nostradamus - The Millennium and Beyond*. New York: Simon & Scuster, 1993. The latest of the illustrated versions, published in 1993, and concerned with the prophecies related to the end of this millennium and the first years of the twenty-first century.

EDGAR CAYCE

Reed, Henry. *Edgar Cayce - The World's Greatest Psychic - On Prophecy.* Various paperback editions. Part of a series of books on the different writings and words of the famous American psychic.

ST. JOHN THE DIVINE

The Book of Revelation, from the King James version of the Bible.

Lorie, Peter. **Revelation - the Prophecies - The Apocalypse and Beyond.** New York: Simon & Schuster.

OTHER PROPHETS AND THEIR WORKS

Anzar, Nadsherwan. *The Beloved: The Life and Works of Meher Baba.* North Myrtle Beach, SC: Sheriar Press, 1974.

Aurobindo, Sri. *The Future Revolution of Man: The Divine Life Upon Earth.* Wheaton, IL: Quest Books, 1974.

Avabhasa, Da (Free John). *The Dawn Horse Testament.* Clearlake, CA: Dawn Horse Press, new standard edition, 1991.

Baba, Meher, and D. E. Stevens, ed. *Listen Humanity.* San Franciso, CA: Harper and Row/Colophon, 1971.

Baigent, Michael; Richard Leigh, and Henry Lincoln. *The Messianic Legacy.* London: Corgi Books, 1987.

Berlitz, Charles. *Doomsday 1999.* New York: Doubleday, 1981.

Bernbaum, Edwin. *The Way to Shambhala: A Search for the Mythical Kingdom Beyond the Himalayas.* Garden City, NJ: Anchor Press/Doubleday, 1980.

John the Divine *from "Les trés riches heures du Duc de Berry," 15th century illuminated manuscript.*

Blavatsky, H.P. *The Secret Doctrine.* Madras, India: Theosophical Publishing House, 1888.

Edmonds, I.G. *Second Sight: People Who Read the Future.* New York: Thomas Nelson Inc. Publishers, 1977.

Free John, Da (Da Avabhasa). *Garbage and the Goddess.* Lowerlake, CA: Dawn Horse Press, 1974.

Free John, Da. *The Enlightenment of the Whole Body.* Middletown CA: Dawn Horse Press, 1978.

Fromm, Erich. *To Have or To Be? A New Blueprint for Mankind.* London: Abacus, 1978.

Hall, Manly P. *The Secret Teachings of All Ages.* Los Angeles, CA: The Philosophical Research Society Inc., 1978.

Jochmans, J.R. *Rolling Thunder The Coming Earth Changes.* Santa Fe, NM: Sun Books/Sun Publishing, 1986, tenth printing.

Krishnamurti, J. *Commentaries on Living.* Wheaton, IL: Quest Books, 1967.

Lawrence, D.H. *Apocalypse.* London: Penguin, 1984.

Mohammed M.H. Shakir, translator. *The Holy Quran.* Elmhurst, New York: Tahrike Tarsile Qur'an, Inc., 1988.

Helena Petrovna Blavatsky

Ouspensky, P.D. *In Search of the Miraculous.* London: Harvest/HBJ Book, 1977.

Rajneesh, Bhagwan Shree. *Beyond Psychology.* Cologne: Rebel Publishing House, 1981.

Rajneesh, Bhagwan Shree. *The Golden Future.* Cologne: Rebel Publishing House, 1987.

Rajneesh, Bhawan Shree. *The Last Testament.* Cologne: Rebel Publishing House, 1986.

Rajneesh, Bhagwan Shree. *The New Man - The Only Hope for the Future.* Cologne: Rebel Publishing House, 1987.

Satprem, Sri Aurobindo: *The Adventure of Consciousness.* New York: Institute for Evolutionary Research, 1970.

Schell, Jonathan. *The Fate of the Earth.* London: Picador, 1982.

Yatri. *Unknown Man; The Mysterious Birth of a New Species.* New York: Simon & Schuster, 1988.

The Garden of Eden, by Erastus Salisbury Field, c.1865. The Shelburne Museum, Shelburne, Vermont. The great dream which appears, as every new millennium approaches, is of a return to a golden age of light, peace and innocence. Will the passing of this old millennium herald such a really new beginning as is forecast?

PICTURE ACKNOWLEDGMENTS

British Museum, London: 7, 18, 20, 30, 35.

Malcolm Godwin: 10, 11, 21, 58, 61, 64, 67, 71, 91-93, 97-101.

Frederiksborg Palace, Denmark: 12.

Science Photo Library, London: {*Erich Schrempp* 13; *Tsuyoshi Nishiinoue* 46; *Doug Allan* 59; *David Parker* 73; *Massonet* 75; *Julian Baum* 81}.

Mary Evans Picture Library, London: 15.

Magnum Photos, London: {*Chris Steele-Perkins* 19; *James Nachtwey* 24; *Hiroji Kubota* 26; *Harry Gruyaert* 66; *Abbas* 69; *Sebastiao Salgado* 96 bottom left; *Bruno Barbey* 96 bottom center; *Gilles Peress* 108; *Steve McCurry* 112}.

Bridgeman Art Library, London: {*Akademie Der Bildenden Kunste, Vienna* 23; *Musee Conde, Chantilly* 34, 118; *Wallraf-Richartz Museum*, Cologne 37; *Museo Di San Marco Dell'Angelico, Florence* 42; *National Trust, Petworth House, Sussex* 83}.

Bibliotheque Nationale, Pàris: 29.

Hulton Deutsch, London: 31, 41, 45, 60. {*Keystone Collection* 77; *Bob McNeely* 79}, 111.

Impact, London: {*Jez Coulson* 32; *Ben Edwards* 57; *Piers Cavendish* 102 inset, 104 bottom center, 104 top left; *Peter Menzel* 115}.

Images Colour Library, London: 38, 65, 84, 96 top.

British Aerospace Defence: 49.

Sygma, London: {*Jon Jones* 50; *Balder* 62, 105 top left, 107; *D. Kirkland* 78; *Giansanti* 88; *Pierre Toutain-Dorbec* 96 bottom right; *Moe Doiron* 104 bottom left; *Richard Melloul* 104 bottom right}.

Museum of Fine Arts, Springfield, MA: 52.

Library of Congress, USA: 54.

Toronto Globe & Mail: 76.

Cesar Pelli & Associates: {renderer: *Lee Dunnette* 94}.

Collections, London: {Anthea Sieveking 103}.

Format Partners, London: {*Joanne O'Brien* 104 top right; *Brenda Prince* 105 top right}.

Shelburne Museum, Vermont: {photo by *Ken Burris* 121}.

Every effort has been made to trace all present copyright holders of the material used in this book, whether companies or individuals. Any ommission is unintentional and we will be pleased to correct any errors in future editions of this book.

ACKNOWLEDGMENTS

The Author would like to acknowledge the work of the following:

Beedham, Brian. ***The World in 1994***—Economist Magazine Supplement. London: Economist Publications, 1993.

Noone, Richard W. ***5/5/2000—Ice. The Ultimate Disaster***. New York: Harmony Books, 1986.

Langley, Noel. ***Edgar Cayce—The World's Greatest Psychic.*** London: The Aquarian Press, Harper Collins, 1989.

Beckley, Timothy Green, and Crockett, Arthur. ***Prophecies of the Presidents—The Spiritual Destiny of America Revealed***. New Jersey: Inner Light Publications, 1984, 1992.

Aburdene, Patricia, and Naisbitt, John. ***Megatrends for Women***. New York: Random House, 1992.

Toffler, Alvin. ***Future Shock***. London: Bodley Head, 1970.

Fisher, Joe. ***Predictions***. London: Sidgewick & Jackson.